CHAMPION
ON THE TABLE

A MEDICAL MEMOIR OF A BRAIN TUMOR SURVIVOR

DR. KENTAYA BEELER

www.CHAMOME.com

Category: Medical Memoir, Self-Help, Personal Finance, Long-Term Care, Tax Deductions

Written by: Dr. Kentaya Beeler | info@chamome.com | 1-800-794-0677

Cover Designed & Formatted by: EliTheBookGuy.com

Printed in the U. S. A.

First Printing, August 2023

Library of Congress Cataloging-in-Publication Data has been applied for.

ISBN: 979-8-9889802-0-9

CONTENTS

FOREWORD

Dr. Candace White

I AM HONORED TO WRITE THIS foreword for my dear friend, Dr. Kentaya Beeler, and her forthcoming medical memoir. This book is a powerful testament to the importance of patient advocacy and the critical role that each of us can play in our own healthcare journeys.

As a board certified primary care physician myself, I have seen firsthand the challenges that patients face in navigating the complex and often overwhelming healthcare system. Too often, patients feel powerless and unheard, as if they are at the mercy of a system that doesn't have their best interests at heart.

Dr. Beeler's story is a powerful reminder that this doesn't have to be the case. Through her own experiences as a patient, she learned the importance of self-advocacy and has developed a wealth of knowledge and practical strategies that can help others do the same.

In this book, Dr. Beeler shares her own journey through the healthcare system, offering a candid and deeply personal perspective on what it means to be a patient in today's world. With warmth, empathy, and a deep sense of compassion, she guides readers through the challenges and pitfalls of the healthcare system, and offers practical advice on how to navigate it with confidence and clarity.

Whether you are facing a serious illness, struggling to get the care you need, or simply looking to be more empowered and informed as a patient, this book is an invaluable resource. I have no doubt that it will inspire and empower readers to take charge of their own healthcare, and to demand the level of care and attention that they deserve.

Thank you, Dr. Beeler, for sharing your story with us. Your courage, strength, and wisdom are an inspiration to us all, and I have no doubt that this book will make a profound difference in the lives of many.

Dr. Candace White

PREFACE

"Okay God, it's just You and me. It's going to be what it is going to be. Either I'm coming home with You or I'm coming back." ~ Dr. Kentaya Beeler

As I made my way down the hall to the operating room, none of the other stuff mattered to me. I was about to enter a fight for my life with no assurances. The doctors did not give me any good news, but I could not just give up on myself.

As the doctors prepped me for the operating table, I realized how much I was distracted by the wrong things. My family was around with me. I could hear my father giving instructions to the doctors. I was his precious baby again after a long period of estrangement. I was grateful to have him there along with my mother and other family members who came out to support me.

The moment that I realized how much I had to live for was also the first time that I truly embraced my mortality. I could make any plans I wanted but first, God had to see me through a life-changing surgery.

That experience and all the adversities that followed changed my perspective on life, relationships, family, and career, among many other things. People look at the past with nostalgia because it reminds them of a time when they still had the bliss that only naivety brings. You remember your childhood fondly because you did not comprehend all the things happening around you and their implications. For example, I did not understand how much my parents' divorce meant and how it affected me until I grew older. That naivety is the reason many of us romanticize the past as well as people, things, and situations that we do not fully understand, even as adults.

Well, the future is a different kind of unknown, and it is the one that we can influence. You don't have to wait for a grand moment like mine to set yourself straight and go for the things that will give you the outcome you hope for in your future.

INTRODUCTION

"I love you. You are the epitome of a fighter. We named you Kentaya from Kunta Kinte. We thought you were a boy, and you came out a girl. You have done everything at this point to be more powerful than if a man had a son." ~ Harry Beeler

LIFE IS NOT A BED OF ROSES, AND MANY PEOPLE LEARN THIS lesson very early in life. Nobody goes through life unscathed. Challenges attempt to define your existence, but you have the final word on how you want to live your life.

I still have a lot of life to live and a lot more lessons to learn. However, one lesson stuck with me from my darkest moments — the will of the human spirit is unbreakable. Sometimes, you don't know how strong you are until you are out of alternatives.

This book does not aim to awe readers with the amount of trauma that I have endured because in my opinion, I have not lived the hardest life. Also, I never glorify hardship because there is nothing to envy in passing through trying times.

Instead, I want everyone who flips through these pages to find the inspiration to face the challenges that they may encounter in their lives with complete confidence. Adversities come in different shapes, colors, and forms. They can be physical, emotional, medical, or psychological. Sometimes, you might have done nothing wrong, that's just how life is.

I know all of this because I have lived through these experiences and I have always found the will to forge ahead within myself. Even when you have the most loving people in your corner, you still have to find within yourself the will to push through.

I hope my story helps you build the mental strength you need to work through the challenges that life throws at you.

LEG 1

PARENTAL DYNAMIC

THE STORY

*"I was taught that it was okay to be different
and be who you are." - Dr. Kentaya Beeler*

My parents are the personification of opposites attracting. My mother was so private, she wouldn't dare give you details about things she didn't want you to know. My father, the firecracker, just didn't care. They met in Saint Petersburg, Florida, and married in my mothers' hometown of Crystal River, Florida in 1975. Their African-style wedding was undeniable proof of their *I'm Black and I'm Proud* mentality. Dressed in Dashikis, they represented our rich history with pride. On the twelfth day of October in 1977, the by-product of their love, me, Kentaya Laquhe' "Sunshine" Beeler was introduced to the world. Delivered at just seven months, I must have been eager to arrive. Premature and weighing only 3 pounds and 2 ounces, I became affectionately known as the "shoebox baby." Due to my size, carrying me in a traditional baby carrier was not possible. It was my mother's neighbor who proclaimed, *"There's no reason to buy an expensive baby carrier because she can fit in a shoebox."* To ensure my vitality, I remained in an incubator at the hospital for approximately two months. And when I met the health requirements to go home with my parents, it was without question they did everything in their power to care for me. My grandmother

Harry and Betty Beeler, 1975

often recounted her memories of stories where my dad spent nights sleeping on the floor near my bassinet to make sure I was breathing. In addition to being premature, I also suffered from asthma and bronchitis as a baby. These stories are the initial chapters of my extensive medical journey.

My mom worked as a Laboratory Technician and Histologist in the hospital making her the perfect advocate for me and my medical care. My parents were both thoughtful and strategic in their approach towards my medical needs. From a young age, I observed what caring for a person should look like. More importantly, I witnessed their effort of unquestionable teamwork. Together they cultivated an environment of love for the baby girl they prayed to conceive. In her true private fashion, my mother held to her bosom the fact that the doctors told her she could not have children, but as the old adage goes, *prayer changes things.*

For the first four or five years of my life, I grew up in a culturally aware household. 9th Street on the Southside of Saint Pete was called the "hood" however the walls of our home were painted with love. In my younger years, my dad was a school bus driver. Oftentimes he picked me up from daycare because he had an early day, and afterwards, he returned home to cook. He prepared meals with love. My dad was multifaceted. In addition to cooking, he also knew how to clean and fold clothes. Due to the hours my mother worked, dad was most often the person I saw initially after school. The music piping from the two sets of headphones plugged into his eight-track player in the garage became the soundtrack for my life. And when we weren't spending quality time together, dad was entertaining guests. Whether as the umpire for the community baseball team, or in other social settings, he was a social butterfly indeed.

In our home, both my mom and dad established a system for parenting and attending to my needs. My mother's job at the hospital required her to leave early in the morning, so she was the person who dropped me off at daycare. By the time my mom got home, my dad would have dinner prepared and the house cleaned. Our family dynamic was potent with love and ingrained in everything I knew.

By the time I was six years of age, my life abruptly changed forever when my parents made the decision to divorce. It was traumatic for me because at that age, I was in this bosom of love and being taught about African pride and the power of the family unit. Their decision to go their separate ways became my first encounter with trauma. My world was shaken at such a young age, and there was a sense of disconnect. For me, their decision and the shift in my life was out of the blue because my parents had not disclosed what was going on.

Although my parents divorced, my mother never seemed to let it impact her mental space. My mother woke me up every day, all the way up to high school, with love in her heart and a melody in her soul.

Every morning she would sing *"Get up, get up, in the morning; Get up, get up in the morning; Get up get up in the mor-ning; It's time to go to school."*

On Sunday mornings, she sang before we prepared to go to church. Every morning, there was a song. As a notable fixer in our family, Mom was known for her warm, and bubbly reassurance that *everything is going to be okay.* A true caregiver to the core, she exemplified quiet strength.

During my critical learning years, her strength became mine and manifested in my educational endeavors with numbers. Math became my claim to fame. Reading however, was not my strong suit. Words atop pages bored me. When my mom noticed this, she started reading the books to me, instead of requesting for me to read aloud. Then we would discuss the books in depth. After she would tell me about the books I would then write about what we discussed. I was a better writer than reader. Although I was weak in my ability to read, mom empowered me to be stronger. This was the way she handled everyone whom she encountered. Although mom was the most powerful, she was not the most heard voice in the room. This made me become more independent. She made it her sole purpose to make sure I was vocal. She instilled the spirit of speaking up in me. She always charged me up by giving me words of encouragement.

She would often say *"You know you can do it"* or *"If this is a challenge, let me help you give extra."*

As an encourager, there was nothing I could not accomplish with her help or in her presence. My mother taught me not only to be a woman, but also to be a fixer. She believed that women don't necessarily have to be heard, to be seen. She taught me about the importance of establishing your home as a haven, and a holistic place. Her messages of independence and self-care were potent. Even after her divorce from my father, and picking up an extra job, I can't recall a time when she talked about being tired. Instead, she often proclaimed, *"I just have to do what I have to do."* As a woman, I learned that we are equipped to adjust to any type of situation in a positive manner. It was this mindset that inspired me to see the best attributes of both my parents.

My dad was my number one supporter. Whether I was right or wrong, his loyalty belonged to me. He was a strong force and at times he lived and loved with an iron fist of persistence. Even if he was wrong, he was going to stick to his disposition till the end. For example, I had asthma, and his opinion was that he didn't want anyone else to chastise me other than him or my mom, because he didn't want me to have an asthma attack. One day in particular, I talked back to one of my aunts who made a decision to spank me. Old enough and aware of my dad's disposition, I resolved to tell my mom what happened. Not only had this rule been set by my father, it was widely known.

When I got home, I informed my mother about my aunt's disciplinary action and she responded *"It's okay."* In my mind it wasn't.

"Nope, I'm gonna tell my dad," I replied.

And when I did, he was livid. He was so angry that we jumped in his car and went back to my aunt's house because in his words "we were going to nip this in the bud."

He made sure to tell her that her spanking me was unacceptable. It did not go over well. Their exchange ended in a physical altercation.

"I already told you not to physically chastise Kentaya. You know she suffers from asthma," he warned.

Boundaries for my father were non negotiable. His ability to set parameters for himself and his family was an attribute that I admired greatly. His disposition and his words implanted in my soul were established as the essence of who and what I became.

On those days he told me, *"You are the most beautiful girl in the world,"* not only did I believe him, but I was inspired to trust in myself and my innate power.

"You are highly intelligent."

"You can do anything a man can do."

If they don't like you, "F" them."

"Go for it!"

"Even if you are the only person going in that direction, you keep going."

These phrases he often repeated were food for my soul. Over the years, he was always on standby to reaffirm me.

Although I had the benefit of the certainty of his words about me, the failed relationship between my mother and father left me with several doubts about whether or not two people had the capacity to stay together. The ending of the union between my mother and father taught me that even the strongest relationships can be broken. My disposition over time became such that relationships are only for a season, and a designated time frame.

The times I had watched my parents together, they were affectionate and displayed their love with hugs and kisses. The same music my dad played for me, he also played for my mom and they danced together on regular days, not just special occasions. In my eyes, they were the epitome of togetherness.

Even outside of our home, their love did not change. Some of my fondest memories of my parents together are centered in the state fair. Atop my dad's shoulders, I felt like I had a window to the world as he held my mother's hand. He was the epitome of what I believed a man to be as we played games and he won various stuffed animals and prizes, only to hand them over to mom and me as sentiments of his affection. I even have pictures of mom and dad at family gatherings. That same affection is memorialized for an eternity. Their love was all I knew, until it ended. The fact that my dad never came back home to live stung in a way that I still can't quite describe. Memories of our childhood are embedded in our emotional DNA and shape our beliefs and the way in which we respond to the events that transpire in our own lives.

Long after my mom and dad's divorce, he came to the house one day. I don't know how long it had been since they parted ways, but he wanted to talk to *me*. Despite him pleading, my mother denied his request.

"No, this is not the time," she responded.

After he left, things were different in the house. Mom even changed the locks. I can recall him being out on the porch, basically screaming that he wanted to see me and wanted to talk to me. My mom was at the window sticking to her guns.

"No this is not the time," she replied once more.

Seeing my father saddened me. I wanted nothing more than to go outside. My mom tried to calm me down while advising me to go back to my room. The entire ordeal upset me. It became this crying and screaming fest between them, until my mom opened the door.

I can remember sitting in the car listening to my dad as he attempted to explain that things were going to be different. His side of the story was that my mom wanted him out of her home. He stated that she left him, and our family would be separated. I was confused and didn't understand what he was saying. What I did know was that he was telling me that it was her and not him. He went on to explain that we wouldn't be doing things as a family the same way we had before. His use of words like visitation and pick up days saddened me as they made my parent's separation real. From the moment I heard him refer to his new place of residence as his house, there was no turning back.

By the time I closed the door of his car in preparation to go back inside, I hated my mom. Based upon the explanation I was given, it was she who caused this disruption of our family. When dad drove off I wanted to go with him, but I knew my mom would not allow for it. By the time I got to the front door, I was in tears. My mom attempted to console me, but I didn't want her near me. An explanation that made sense was what I was after. I wanted to know why she caused our family pain. The fact that she didn't have a solid answer, made me more furious. For days after my father's visit, I waited for her to say something—anything that would make sense. After that day, it took awhile for us to establish a new normal, one that didn't involve my dad living under the same roof with us. Instead of doing things together on weekends, we began a routine of visiting my mom's family in Crystal River, Florida. During that time, I got to enjoy exchanges with family members and cousins of the same age, which was exciting.

The establishment of this routine was the start of a new sense of normalcy. Being around other kids my age and not being the only young person was exciting to me.

Eventually, my dad moved across the street with my uncle. On the days he picked me up from school, we hung out like old times. The only difference now was that I never spent the night. My dad didn't want me spending the night. It wasn't as if my uncle would do anything to me, it was just that their home was more of a bachelor pad. Over time, I adjusted to our new normal and made it my own. In fact, it felt cooler because it was like I had two houses.

He lived across the street up until I was in the 6th grade. Everything changed again after he got remarried and made the decision to move out of town with his new wife. It was the end of an era. My relationship with my father took a turn for the worse because I felt abandoned. It was as if he just left one day. He never disclosed to me that he was moving. He just left. He told me that his plan was to pick me up on weekends, but that was inconsistent. Some weekends he wouldn't make it. I can recall a scattered series of Saturdays sitting in the window, dressed and waiting for his arrival for hours on end. It crushed me. The times I attempted to inquire why he didn't come, he would tell me that his wife and her kids had something to do and he needed to help them. In my heart, I felt as though he traded me for this other family. I was no longer prioritized in my father's life and it hurt like hell. All I had ever known was how to be his everything, but after he remarried, I felt like I was only an option. Everything changed. Even my view of him changed. No longer did I see him as a strong and powerful man. It seemed like he lost himself and became the opposite of who he used to be.

The aha moment for me was in learning that for an extended period of time, I failed to see my mom for who she truly was. I realized that for so long, I had this bad and biased view about her based on my dad's story about their divorce. In full transparency, I despised my mom for making me lose my dad. I blamed her for everything. It was not until he remarried, I was empowered to see the forest from the trees. Seeing this other side of my father, allowed me to begin understanding that it wasn't my mom's fault he moved out. I was also now old enough to understand that they had their issues, and it wasn't my place to pick sides. My relationship with my mom evolved with realization. For the first time in a very long time, I saw the strength of the woman that I came from. It was a strength that I would need in the years to come.

THE LESSON

I learned a lot from my parents as an only child. They took their time to instill a lot of life lessons into me. As an adult, the most profound lesson that largely impacts my life is remaining positive through all things. Despite what my parents were going through, they did not allow it to affect how they raised me. Not all parents know how to do that. Most times, when couples are going through a rough patch in their relationship, you will first notice it in the kids. Some kids end up as truants or are just unhappy. In my heart, I appreciate how my parents put my happiness first. Never did I notice what they were going through, hence the divorce being a shock to me.

As I got older, there were times my dad did disappoint me when he didn't show up to visit as he promised. Left with no other choice, I was forced to find the silver lining.

Some say that there is a reason for everything, and I do agree. While we may not always like the series of events that take place in our lives, the end result is always rewarding. Watching my parents get divorced taught me about how I desired to shape

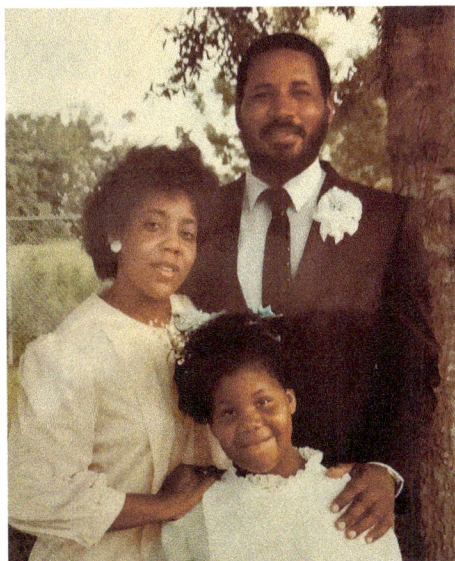

my family when I had one. My mother's teachings on having a voice and being a woman and my dad's cheerfulness and love for his child will forever be ingrained in my mind. While they were not able to make their relationship work, they succeeded in raising a strong person who personified strength.

" LOVE WITH ALL YOUR HEART AND
BE THE BEST VERSION OF YOURSELF
NO MATTER THE CIRCUMSTANCES. "

LEG 2

THE JOURNEY OF EDUCATION

THE STORY

*"For every stage of life, there are one or more hurdles
you will have to tackle, and you need someone to talk
to through every hurdle." - Dr. Kentaya Beeler*

I REMEMBER BEING IN MIDDLE SCHOOL WITH A MATH teacher named Mr. Moore who really didn't get why his class was not harmonious. He was complaining about it. I was pretty quiet in school and got good grades. I remember speaking up about it. One day I just said, *"Mr. Moore, it's not that we don't like the material, it's just that we don't like your attitude."* I got put out of the classroom. I wasn't one of the disruptive ones. I wasn't throwing balls in the classroom, but he said I had a very persnickety attitude. So I guess that day in my quietness, I felt fed up in my champion spirit and felt that I needed to clarify for him why he had such problems in the class. Of course, it led to an in-school suspension and my mother had to come. She really had to explain to me that the problem wasn't my battle. If I wasn't the one causing trouble,

I didn't have to speak. He really said to me that he kicked me out of the class because I was very disrespectful, and I couldn't wrap my mind around that. I didn't do anything. I just provided clarity. We had a very strange relationship for the rest of that term. My mother had to come out to the school again because my grading was very subjective, and I had never had grades like that before. So I always remembered that experience, and my mother did too. I later realized that he believed that I disrespected his authority because I said something that hurt his character.

> In many instances, pre-existing conditions allow medical staff to rule out proper diagnoses.

High school, to me, felt like I was elevating in my excellence. I participated in all the activities and joined many organizations. I loved high school and really got to be who I was. It was in high school I discovered accounting and started developing an interest in the subject. I originally wanted to be a statistician but after a trip to NASA, that dream was cut short. I remember it being boring and cold. When we had to discuss what we wanted to be, I had no idea what I wanted to be after that NASA visit. One day I was talking to a teacher who asked me if I knew about accounting and the industries that need accountants. I said *"No, I had never tried it before."* She told me about the Future Business Leaders of America program. I joined her auditing class and I loved it. From there, I knew I wanted to be an accountant.

The only school I applied to was Florida A&M University (FAMU). I was very confident in getting accepted. I knew since middle school what college I would attend, and I made sure from that time on to do what I needed to do to get in. When I finally got accepted, I remember taking my letter right up to the College Acceptance Letter Board that we had in the high school and adding mine. That was a time I really celebrated. I started planning my trunk party and getting my orange and green dishes (FAMU's colors). It was really exciting going to college, especially since a lot of other students from my school were going as well. I also had a lot of family that lived in Tallahassee, so I didn't feel like I was that far from home.

The first day that I got there, I was anxious and nervous because I was used to being an only child. I was nervous about having to share and be in a tiny place. That feeling quickly dissipated at the sight of the Omegas, who were helping us move in. I remember their bodies glistening with sweat and their chiseled physique peeking out of their cut-up purple shirts. As they moved my things into Cropper Hall, I continued to be mesmerized by their blunt masculinity that was standing firm in their gold boots. Getting to my room allowed for continued excitement. Being first in the room, I was able to pick the side I desired. From there, my college journey continued. Going to class wasn't strange for me since I was able to participate in the Tops Program that summer. All my classes were already chosen and set up, so the last thing I needed to do was meet my roommate. So I thought.

That first week of classes, my mother stayed with me. On the first day of class, she walked me to class and attempted to give her number to the professor, just in case they "had any problems with me." The professor politely informed my mom that I was an adult and calling her when I had a problem wasn't done in college. My mother, the nurturer, still remained in the building outside of my class until I was done. She actually stayed that entire week and finally left that Sunday. To my surprise, as I saw her car disappear in the horizon further away from the back of the building, reality set in that I was indeed now an adult. I was 17 and on my own. I immediately had an emotional breakdown. Others tried to console me but to no avail. After all, what was I going to tell them? I miss my mommy and I want to go home? That was embarrassing. I just sucked it up until the following weekend when I went home, but my mother wasn't having it. I remember her telling me *"Nope, you wanted to go so bad! You can't be coming home every weekend."* I ended up joining some on-campus activities. One was a dorm step team called TWC. That really helped me get acclimated to other people and not make me miss home so much. That was very beneficial to me because I also no longer wanted to rush back and be with my high school boyfriend, who I also left back home. Joining TWC really helped me stay focused on school. Eventually my relationship did suffer as my boyfriend ended up cheating on me and getting someone else pregnant. What I learned in that hurtful situation was that another man's love was temporary. I had no choice but to walk into this newness, and it was okay being around different people. What I had back home needed to be updated, and me being in school and around other people helped me. School became a coping mechanism. TWC was like a sorority, and

I was able to connect with other girls who were having the same experiences.

Freshman year did end up being very tough. My grandmother lived in Crystal River, Florida, which connected Florida US 19 Highway to Tallahassee Apalachee Parkway. That was a stop I always made on my way back to school, including after winter break in 1995. My mother and I stopped by my grandmother's house. While there, my grandmother showed us that something bit her while she was hanging up clothes outside. Crystal River is in the countryside of West Central Florida so there are a lot of insects. I remember her showing the bite to me. It was swollen and liquidy. My mother said *"Oh, you might have to have that lanced."* My grandmother said *"Okay."* My mom took me back to school and told me that she was going back to check on my grandmother because she didn't like the way her leg looked. By the end of that first week of the spring 1996 semester, my grandmother was hospitalized. They confirmed that she was bitten by something but didn't take it seriously because of her **diabetes**. The doctors were under the impression that she wasn't healing because of her diabetes. They were going to lance it and do a procedure. At the time, I was not familiar with diabetes or how it affected her health. The following week, my grandmother died.

> **DIABETES** is a chronic, metabolic disease characterized by abnormal levels of blood glucose (or blood sugar), which leads over time to serious damage to heart, blood vessels, kidneys, and nerves.

A **PRE-EXISTING CONDITION** is a known illness, injury, or health condition that exists before a new health event.

Chamomè, LLC.
Webinars including
Grief **Counseling**

It was discovered that she was bitten by a poisonous brown recluse spider. She wasn't healing because of the poison from the spider taking over her system. My grandmother's story is proof of the fact that there is and has always been a need for thorough testing, self-advocacy, and healthcare surrogates to ensure proper care.

I returned back to school after the funeral. My grandmother's death was a traumatic experience in part because I was unable to call my then ex-boyfriend who also knew her. I was hit with my grandmother's death and the breakup with my boyfriend in the same school year. For me, it was like experiencing two deaths. From there, my grades just tanked. I recall that after the funeral, I had to go through **counseling**. During the funeral, I bent down to kiss her while she was in the casket, feeling her ice cold and hard texture on my lips. This was my first experience with death and while I knew she would be cold, it didn't process in my mind how cold. So, I went to go kiss her, expecting the warmth that you get when you encounter your grandparents and instead got the coldness. My mind took a snapshot. When I was back on campus, I would see her face when I tried to sleep. My mother ended up coming and spending two weeks with me. My roommate had left because she had some issues, so I was by myself. In the counseling sessions, I talked about this being my first experience with death and it came out that I was experiencing two major deaths — the death of a relationship and the death of my grandmother. Two people in my life that I was emotionally connected to.

My grades were terrible because I could not focus, yet it was better for me not to go home and deal with the fact that my high school love was planning for his baby to arrive. Being in school helped me because I had extra-curricular activities to dip myself into to forget what I was going through. After homecoming, we didn't step again until April. March was when we started practicing again, but I dedicated January and February to focus on my mental health. That time was about me getting the energy to get out of bed, go to the therapy office on campus, and get to my classes. By summer, I had a good amount of therapy completed and my mental health was better. I went back home for an internship during the summer. I was glad to be home and be with my mom and to work and feel relieved. I knew that I needed to recharge because that semester I got all D's and a C. I knew that I needed to get my mind together to get back to school in the fall and make up for what I did. I took a class at Saint Petersburg College with my mother, who decided to go back to college. We took speech together. That was a time for us to re-energize each other.

By the end of summer, I was ready to go back to school because I had a plan. Most of my instructors had reached out to me because they knew what I was going through. They had emailed me and asked what time I wanted to go to class. So,

I was ready to return to campus. Having a support system is important. The summer going into my junior year was pretty uneventful. I was in Tallahassee and took summer classes. At the beginning of the fall semester, I decided to run for student government as the Junior Senator. It was exciting for me because it was the first time I was going to go from doing extra-curricular activities like the step team to actually going to something more purposeful and academic driven. I wanted to run for Junior Senator because I decided I wanted to be a liaison between the student body and administration and ascertain the things that the student body wanted to do on campus. The campaigning process was not easy and resulted in a run-off election but in the end, I won. The senators traveled with the football team during the fall, which was very fun because we got to recruit other students to attend FAMU. We did college fairs and participated around those games. Junior year was really good. I began my upperclassman courses in the School of Business and really found my groove in college. That year truly prepared me for my career in accounting and I felt more purposeful.

Junior year wasn't one of emotional battles for me. I wasn't going through any personal relationships at that point and everything else surrounding me was good. Senior year was the same way. Going into the spring semester, I found out there was one class I needed that was not offered on campus. I decided to take that class at Florida State University (FSU), and it was a culture shock. The auditing class was different. There wasn't a lot of camaraderie. At FAMU, we helped each other and did study groups. I felt ostracized at FSU. There weren't a lot of people who looked like me in the auditing class. The structure of the course was also different. There were three tests, and I am not a great test-taker. I am more of an application person so, I stressed a lot in that class. The class concluded and all roads led to graduation, which I celebrated with my family. Some even traveled to Florida from out of state. After graduation, the celebration continued at Disney World.

A few days later, I discovered that I received a D for that auditing class, not the passing grade I needed for my accounting degree. I ended up going back to FAMU for that one class, and it was very embarrassing. The other students were puzzled because there I was, this recent graduate, still in their class. I had to explain that my urgency to finish my degree and deciding to go to FSU for the auditing class didn't turn out as planned, and that I was in their class because I didn't pass the class with a C or better. Furthermore, I had to explain to my perspective employer that I couldn't move forward with the job offer because of the class grade that meant my degree was not conferred. Basically, my plans after college were placed on hold. I remember being angry at the teacher because I communicated with him from the beginning about only needing that specific class to graduate and having a job offer. I told him about my struggle with taking tests but he was not receptive and very nonchalant. In no way did he hint that I was not passing the class.

That fall was a roller coaster of emotions. I was only in Tallahassee for that one class and my main focus was getting in and getting out. I began doubting myself and didn't like my appearance. I had gained a lot of weight. Perhaps it was because I'd lived off campus a few years and was getting less exercise due to one of my most embarrassing moments of falling on campus and having a hematoma form on my knee. I had limited mobility so no more step team for me. In addition to the weight gain, I realized I often experienced blurry vision and frequent urination. After visiting the doctor, I heard that word again: Diabetes. The doctor diagnosed me as being pre-diabetic and told me that I needed to make some lifestyle changes. Because I was focusing on graduating, healthy eating took a back burner to the late-night study sessions and affordable college budget meals that frequently were not healthy choices. However, my hard work paid off academically and my degree ended up being conferred in December after I passed the class at FAMU. It had more components going into the grading than just three tests. This helped me. I tell students now, *"Don't stay in a class if you are failing."* I was so focused on graduating, I didn't drop the class and failed. Unfortunately, professors are not obligated to structure their class to your learning style. Sometimes, we have to bow out gracefully. Trust the process and wait!

THE LESSON

People have different experiences in school. While some have it good and some bad, it was mixed for me. Getting into college and choosing a program of study was quite easy because I had everything figured out early. I know most people face the issue of deciding which program to study and which school to attend, but it was different for me. I thought college was going to be easy throughout because I had an easy start, but things changed. I think that's what being an adult is all about. Sometimes we have it so easy that we think everything is going to keep going well then all of a sudden, something bad like losing a family member or going through a heartbreak happens. Then it becomes a rollercoaster of bad things. I have come to understand that knowing things won't always be rosy saves us from drowning when things go bad. This is what differentiates a realist from an optimist or pessimist. As a realist, you don't expect things to always be bad or good. You understand that life is a mixture of both. I wish someone had told me this when I got into college. Maybe then I would have been able to live through the bad days without letting it affect my studies. At the end of the day, therapy did get me back on track.

I always tell people they need someone to talk to. It could be their family, friends, or a therapist. For me, talking to a therapist in college when I lost my grandmother worked because my mom was also going through the pain of losing her mom. For every stage of life, there are one or more hurdles you will have to tackle, and you need someone to talk to through every hurdle. Talking to my mom when I got suspended in middle school helped me to understand what I did wrong and get over it. Talking to a therapist in college helped me to heal from the pain of losing my boyfriend and my grandmother. Over the years, talking to people has helped me heal, grow, and remain positive. Talking to someone you trust helps. Take note of the word "trust" here, because sometimes talking to the wrong people can make things worse. If you have a good circle of friends you can talk to and rely on, that's great. If you have a close-knit family, that's super great. But if you don't, it is also cool to talk to a therapist and get help. You can't do life alone!

"I UNDERSTAND THAT THINGS WON'T ALWAYS GO THE WAY I WANT, AND I WILL EXPERIENCE SOME BAD DAYS, BUT I WILL NOT LET THEM BRING ME DOWN. I WILL TALK TO SOMEONE WHEN I HAVE TO."

LEG 3

A NEW BEGINNING IN THE BIG APPLE

THE STORY

*"There was nothing other than God's timing
and God's grace that stopped me from
being dead..." ~ Dr. Kentaya Beeler*

I MOVED TO NEW YORK ONCE MY DEGREE WAS CONFERRED, although I lost all initial job opportunities due to having to repeat the auditing course. I arrived on a one-way ticket that my cousin bought for me. I had two aunts there and my grandmother's sister. Their advice to me was that I was in the financial capital of the world and coming there with an accounting degree would guarantee me a job. But I had to hit the pavement, and that was what I did. I left for New York on January 3, 2000. I already set up appointments with Robert Half & Account Temps. I had an interview that Monday, and I started working that Thursday in a temp position. New York was not unfamiliar territory. My cousins and I enjoyed visiting different states during the holidays. We would switch summers in between Florida and New York. However, being in

New York and working was much different than just hanging out there in the summer. The personalities and culture were very different for me. Down South, we are very hospitable. I remember going into work in New York and I said *"Good morning everyone."* One lady was like *"Is it?"* I was taken aback. I'm like *"Yeah it is,"* and she told me *"You come into work too excited and chipper. We aren't like that here."* This was the response I would get quite often and this lasted during my entire stay in New York. That part was challenging.

I also learned about the different minority classes. A lot of people in NY have some type of mixed heritage. So while they may have a darker hue, they could be Dominican, Panamanian, or Guianese. A lot of people wanted to know what I was because you get treated a certain way or respected a certain way based on your heritage. I would let it be known that I am Black, and I don't have any mixed heritage. To me it was like, *"What does that matter?"* In Florida, Black people are *Black people.* I did find out that classism of culture existed in New York even though it's supposed to be a melting pot. Nuances like my accent would be mocked. I didn't experience that in Florida. I thought it was very ignorant.

Career wise, I advanced very quickly in New York. My temporary position turned into a permanent position and after 11 months, I transferred to a subsidiary of the Department of Treasury as an auditor of banks. I know for sure that if I had been in the South, I would not have been given that opportunity that quickly, especially being African American and not having a lot of experience. I learned a lot in regard to work ethic. I remember the days when I still had to go to work even if there was a snowstorm. The workday wasn't canceled because of snow as a New Yorker. You knew to park your car at the train station, put on your sneakers, and tote your heels in your carrying bag until you got to work. My total stay in New York was from 2000 to 2004. I was there during 9/11 and the New York blackouts — two traumatic events let me know that New York was not for me!

September 11 was a very difficult day. At that time, the work I was doing required me to be in multiple places doing bank audits. That particular day, I was headed toward the World Trade Center stop because I had an assignment in lower Manhattan. Fortunately, I was running late that day, but I was on the train. I remember the brakes being put on the train, which screeched in a way I had never heard before. The voice of the conductor traveled through each car. "*Everybody off, everybody off.*" We were in between stations, and they told all of us to get off. We had to walk in the subway underground tunnel. We didn't know what was going on, but what we knew was that it was an emergency and they were telling us to get off the train. I had a lot of papers with me as well as a bag with my heels in them and sneakers on my feet. We were walking wanting to know what was going on. We came up to the street level and at that point, we were uptown above the World Trade Center. I noticed people who were dirty, and I didn't quite understand. They made us all get on city buses that were lined up. We got on the bus and people were crying. Some of us assumed that they were crying because of the pandemonium that was going on.

There was a lot of scurrying and whistling. We were trying to figure out what was happening. People started to notice that their cellphones were not working and at that point, we were really curious and wondering what the problem was. All of a sudden, the bus stopped and the driver told us to get off the bus. I asked him, *"What is going on?"* and he said, *"They say we're getting bombed like Pearl Harbor."* There went my champion spirit! I asked him, *"Why would you let us off the bus?"* because it moved faster than we would on foot. He said he was just following orders. He had to go back and get others. At that moment, I became fearful. From what he was telling me, they were bombing NYC and we were still in the Manhattan area. First responders were walking, and they were telling us to walk uptown toward the Bronx to get out of NYC. I remember people running past me with debris on them. It looked like chalk. I got so winded, I sat down at a bus stop. There was a man there with an old portable TV. He was like, *"Okay, here is what is going on."* So we all crowded around him and watched what we thought was a replay of the first plane going into the first tower, but it was actually the second plane going into the second tower. I saw the second tower get hit on live TV. Instant pandemonium ignited. At that point, we just took off running. That moment was when I started crying because in my mind, planes were dropping bombs!

I started running and my asthma was flaring, but I needed to make it out of New York City alive. I had no asthma pump on me because as I got older, my asthma had gotten better. I didn't have to daily medicate with a nebulizing treatment and asthma pump as I did during my childhood. I was diagnosed with exercise-induced asthma with infrequent attacks that could be years apart. Having no medicine or breathing help at that

Who is your **EMERGENCY CONTACT**?

moment was tough. While I was running, I began to think, *"If I die here, who would they call? How would they know my* **emergency contact***? Keep breathing deeply Kentaya. You got to make it out of New York City!"*

Then my secondary instinct kicked in and prompted me to call *my mommy.* I realized that she was probably seeing this and wondering where I was because I never was working in one space. I got out my phone and dialed. My phone was actually working. I called her job and usually it was a switchboard and I had to be transferred to someone who would locate her in the lab. This time, my mom was the one who answered. The immediate relief that transferred through the phone between us was electrifying. She asked me if I was okay and I remember saying *"Yes, I'm okay but…"* The phone cut off. Desperate and scared, I screamed through the phone *"Hello? Hello?"* The people who were running around me caught wind that I had phone service. They started to bombard me for my phone.

I Keep It All Together Project

I remember people yelling at me to use my phone and despite me trying to explain that my call dropped, they still insisted. It wasn't until I opened my flip phone to show the no service signal that they would leave me alone.

I continued to run and then I heard a chirp. Yes, I had a Nextel phone with a walkie-talkie feature. It was my cousin.

37

She asked where I was. I was hyper and crying saying, I didn't know. She told me straight up, *"Listen, get it together and tell me where you are."* She was saying this because she made it to the Bronx, and she was in an area where the police were going to let her stay if I could get to the Bronx as well. So I calmed down and looked around to see what area I was in. People were mobbing me for my phone, but I got a chance to put it in my pocket and found out I was on Street 200 uptown and something, which wasn't far from the Bronx. I took the phone out carefully to chirp my cousin and tell her. She said *"Great, keep going."* I kept walking several more blocks until I got to this church. *"Won't God give you a sign?"* It was a Catholic school with a flagpole and cement steps that I stopped at because my body couldn't run any further. There was this little lady, pushing a shopping cart, and I asked her *"Where am I?"* She said *"Baby, you are in the Bronx."* That was all I wanted to hear. I got to the steps on the building and I collapsed and sat down. Relief.

I chirped my cousin as I sat on the steps. She answered, and I told her I made it to the Bronx. While panting and barely breathing, there was a sigh of relief. I thought to myself, *"You are a champion girl. You made it out of New York City alive!"* I told her where I was and as we were on the phone, I heard the officer in the background giving her the directions on where I could meet her. It was a bit further than the church but after I rested, I felt much better walking. The location where I had to meet her was filled with barricades. Just over the horizon and through the commotion, I saw my cousin's head and her car. She was waving her hands to get my attention. I walked over to her car, got in, and immediately broke down. I let everything out. She drove me to my aunt's house, where I was living. When I got home, I found out my best friend at the time and uncle were able to get home after also being in NYC.

After it all, we had a week of zero internet connection. I wasn't able to talk to my mom for about eight days, though I was able to chirp through the Nextel phones. I can honestly say that during that time, after watching the news and listening to all those who had lost their lives, I realized that had my train been on time, it would have gone through the World Trade Center stop. That freaked me out. I was grateful. That day taught me that the people of NYC are resilient. After two weeks, everyone was back to work. They didn't let the attack stop them. Personally, I felt more blessed. I never took life for granted, but I definitely was more aware about my faith in God. Knowing that He can protect me from seen and unseen dangers was not just a scripture in the Bible. That could have easily been me. There was nothing other than God's timing and God's grace that stopped me from being *dead* because I was in NYC and going to work just like everyone else, and my train was indeed going through that stop.

I continued to work for my company after that and everything was good until I experienced the blackouts. I never had such an experience where I lost complete use of electricity for a week. There was a lot of looting and breaking in of homes in our neighborhood. I remember my uncle and male cousin would take guard at night with guns because people were breaking into homes. The day before the blackout, I was auditing a bank at a prison and the lights went out. They had generators so that little failure didn't make me think it was anything big. While I was there, they asked if anyone had a flashlight, and I told them *"Yes, I do, in my car."* I gave them my flashlight, not knowing that request was an indication we were going to lose all electricity. The way people were acting without having electricity or food was insane. It went from us doing cookouts and enjoying our neighbors to people really becoming desperate and breaking into homes. This taught me survival of the fittest. Some people would judge those who were stealing, but they were actually trying to survive. The situation was really scary for me. I heard about people getting shot and beat to death because they were breaking in and looting. So between 9/11 and the blackouts, I was really questioning whether or not I was cut out for the New York life. I saw a lack of humility in the people. Yes, they were resilient, but their "get up and keep it moving" mentality also caused a lack of humility and I wasn't familiar with that, coming from down South. We would crumble at some of the things they went through.

A real pivot for me was when I broke my knee. I was running up the stairs at home and my knee bent backwards instead of forward. I had the worst recovery, during which I slipped on ice with my crutches. My ability to heal wasn't good because I was diabetic. I was diagnosed as pre-diabetic in college, and the disease progressed to Type 2 diabetes. Unfortunately, I broke my knee during the winter, and I fell multiple times on ice and in the snow. Having surgery in the cold wasn't good for my bones or for a person with an endocrine disease. To add to the difficulty, my job was not flexible at all. At that point,

I was convinced that I was not cut out for this. I decided that I was going to use my time off from work to accelerate my master's degree program and relocate back to Florida. I no longer wanted to be in New York. However, during this time, I met a new love. Leaving him was going to be hard. This is how life works! I was shopping with my cousin when he and I met. He was the manager of the store. I remember the day vividly because she begged me to get out of the house and stretch my knee. I was on crutches just for the day so I could prepare for my knee surgery. She felt taking me out would strengthen my knee. Despite my horrible accident and the recovery I was going through, meeting him opened me up to courting again. He was very encouraging after my surgery by taking me out to rehabilitate my knee. He was also a great encourager and supported me in achieving my master's degree. I was off of work for three or four months and in that time, I focused on rehab and school.

Deciding to leave New York was a big step. Not only was I traumatized but when it came to the cost of living and the personalities surrounding me, I knew it wasn't going to be a long stay. I decided to get my master's in taxation at NOVA Southeastern University in Florida. I still wanted to be in the accounting realm, but I had more of a love for taxation and wanted to see where that would lead me in my career path. It wasn't really an exit strategy from New York but deciding to have another degree under my belt would give me more opportunities, wherever they would take me. As I began drawing closer to ending my master's program, I accepted a job to move to Orlando, Florida.

THE LESSON

I think I can boldly say that since I survived New York, I can survive anywhere. Some of the hardest lessons many young adults have to learn is that things won't always go the way they want. There are many unforeseen circumstances that will happen and ruin some of your plans, and you can't expect to stay in one position for a long time. You may have a great five-year plan right now, and believe me, there is nothing wrong with having a good plan, But prepare for the unforeseen. This way, when things don't go the way you planned, you can get over it quickly. You should also be determined not to remain in one position for the rest of your life. If I wanted to live a mediocre life, I would have stayed put where I was comfortable, stopped studying after my bachelor's degree, or stayed at one job. But I needed to be more, and I knew that meant I needed to put myself out there. Moving to New York was me getting out of my comfort zone and putting myself out there. Of course, I didn't like it much there, but I learned a lot of lessons that have shaped me into the strong person I am today. My 9/11 experience, the blackout, and some other crazy New York events made me stronger than I would ever have been if I stayed put in the South. Sometimes, you need to challenge yourself by trying new things or changing your location.

"I WILL LEAVE MY COMFORT ZONE AND BE MORE. I REFUSE TO BE MEDIOCRE!"

LEG 4

BACK HOME TO FLORIDA I GO

THE STORY

"One thing I have come to understand about marriage is that the moment one party stops fighting for the marriage to work, everything goes to shambles. I have realized that the two people in the relationship have to work together to make sure it works. It's not a one man or one woman thing." ~ Dr. Kentaya Beeler

THE LAST SIX MONTHS BEFORE GOING HOME WERE ALL about preparation. My mom flew to New York to help me move. We put my car on the Amtrak auto train in Virginia. I wasn't nervous this time around like when I moved to New York on a one-way plane ticket. Knowing there was a job waiting for me in Florida and my family back home was very calming. I remember the train ride back being very relaxing. It was my first time seeing a different side of Amtrak. Of course, I had ridden the train before, but this time I was in the elite car, and it was such a great feeling. My mother and I were in the sleeper car with turn-down service, five-course meals, and movies with equally excited families who were traveling to Florida for Disney. It felt good to be going back home in a more tranquil way and around people who were excited to go to a place that I was returning to.

When I got to Florida, I drove to Orlando in my car after getting off the train. My mother had a classmate in the Orlando area, so we stayed with her while we were there. We also checked out some new apartments. Within a week, I secured an apartment and put everything I transported in my car from New York in the apartment. During that week, I was on break from school and had about one more week before I started my new job, so I was able to really get settled and gather things for my new apartment. My transition was really easy. Once I was settled, it was time to start my new job.

Starting work in a new place was exciting, especially with the presence of my fellow FAMU alumni. There were a lot of African Americans in the construction company, and it felt more like home. It was an environment I was used to although I transferred from banking to the construction industry. I was still an auditor, but I traveled by plane instead of by car compared to my work life in New York. Although I was settling in Orlando and it felt like home, I soon realized that I wouldn't be home that much. Within a month, I was up and about traveling the country for work. I started in New Orleans and Houston, and though it wasn't a lot of snow tracking, it was a lot of air mileage. Originally it was fun, and I saved a lot of money because the company paid for all of my expenses from door to door, which was different from New York. There the cost of living was a bit expensive, and the company I worked for had different benefits when it came to traveling. The job in Florida offered more in that sense, and it made it exciting to travel around, until I started to feel that burnout. I experienced it a lot quicker than I did in New York.

I was also on my way to building a new family with the man that I loved. In December of that year, the guy I had met in New York and was dating decided to come out and spend Christmas with me. He was a father with a daughter, whom I originally met when she was seven months old. He thought it would be a great experience for him and her to come out to Orlando and go to the theme parks. It was his plan to really make a vacation out of it since she lived with her mom in Georgia. We decided to start the vacation off by introducing my mom to his daughter. That day he arrived with the baby was a real transition for me. Once we reached my mom's house from the airport, I told my mom the baby felt warm and appeared to have a high fever while being very agitated. We assumed she needed her diaper changed. When I went to change her diaper, I realized that she did not have on a baby diaper but a maternity pad secured with tape. Her private area was inflamed, enlarged, and infected due to a lack of care. In tears, my mom and I decided to take her to urgent care. When I got there, I informed them that she wasn't my biological child and that she came to me in her present condition. After being seen by the doctor, Urgent Care informed us that the baby girl was suffering from neglect. Her diapers weren't changed regularly as they should have been. She had a wound on her leg from a spider bite that was not attended to and that was causing her fever. The Urgent Care staff did give us a remedy, and we had to pay out of pocket because the baby was insured under her mother's Medicaid benefits in Georgia, which did not transition to Florida.

Do you know if your insurance coverage is state specific and if you are traveling are their medical coverage limitations?

That whole experience changed my life drastically. That Christmas vacation with someone I dated and left in New York, who I loved, turned into a conversation about him relocating to Florida and us taking in his daughter. As a woman, I was pissed that any woman would allow their daughter to be subjected to that amount of pain and neglect. I felt the responsibility to put my singleness and fancy life to the side and actually be serious enough to help take care of this little girl and allow them to come live with me. The talk that he and I had was filled with emotion, and I felt empathy and sympathy for them both. Empathy from the standpoint that he was in mental pain and the baby was in physical pain. Sympathy because I knew the difficulty of this transition for the baby losing the chemical connection with her mom, which would be a lot moving to Florida with us, even though the transition was prompted by neglect by the biological mother. I didn't get a chance to actually talk with her, but I was made aware of the conversation he eventually had with her. Oftentimes, society paints motherhood as a picture of perfection and sheer bliss, but that was far from the truth with this young woman. She admitted to being overwhelmed with the baby and motherhood being too difficult for her at that time. She confessed that she did not want the child. There wasn't anything to debate. The neglect was proof of what her own words revealed. The only thing left to do on our end was to make a plan.

In hindsight, I realize that I didn't see any conflict despite my job being 80% travel because he was there. We discussed how things would be covered financially until he found a job in Florida, where she would be enrolled in school, and we just went into action. He traveled back to New York to get his things and took the baby with him since his mother was there to help keep her. It was the end of January when she was fully enrolled in daycare in Orlando, and we were officially living together. It was a time that actually felt good for me. I wasn't just focusing on business, school, and degrees. I was with someone I loved and enjoyed. Yes, he had a baby, but I didn't have to deal with baby mama drama. We were able to actually be together as a family. Nine months after they moved to Orlando with me, he and I got married. We only told a few people because we just went to the Justice of the Peace. This was to be temporary until we could afford the wedding of my dreams and the heart-shaped diamond ring I envisioned. Essentially, it was a secret wedding that I was okay with because I didn't want to live in sin. I was experiencing true joy. The only thing bringing a cloud over my presumed perfection was the continued conflict in my schedule. I knew I could not be an effective mother and now wife with the work routine that I had.

Being away from home Sunday through Thursday, and even sometimes Friday, didn't create the effectiveness I thought it would. Though I would do my best to make it home on Friday before noon to give him a break, it was still a difficult set up. This was over a two-year period before I transferred to an accounting firm in my third year in Orlando. By that time, I graduated with my master's degree and had become a tax accountant instead of a traveling auditor. However, being a part of the firm and a tax accountant was not what I envisioned. I discovered billable hours and ended up working 14-hour days in order to meet my billable budget for the accounting firm. So despite being local, I didn't spend a lot of time at home. This became another added drain because it was as if I wasn't home *again*, so I became a subject matter tax expert, which cut my working hours down. Once I finally transitioned to being more at home, the clouds cleared and reality began to surface even more.

Home with the family still didn't feel like home with the family as our marriage became plagued with petty little arguments about my role as a mother and wife. All of a sudden, I was at home with these newfound expectations for cooking and cleaning that I wasn't used to. I did start doing those things but since he was so burned out, he was looking for major relief and an opportunity to grow himself. I discovered that he was not a permanent resident of the United States. The issue of the expiration of his passport became another strain on our marriage. I did feel a sense of betrayal that he was not transparent about his residency status, and that was the last thing we needed in our marriage. It wasn't until 2007 when I was given the opportunity to be an adjunct professor that I realized being an educator would give me the time I needed to spend with my family. I transitioned from the certified public accounting firm to full-time higher education as a professor of accounting.

In the process of transitioning, my mom got sick with a condition that was unknown at the time. She was losing five pounds a week and it was speculated that she had cancer, which led me to travel approximately two hours every night from Orlando to Saint Petersburg because she lived alone. Her medical ailments worsened, requiring her to have frequent office visits. The first operation she had, the results came back inconclusive. They had no solution as to why she had the rapid weight loss, felt fatigued, and was struggling to get back to 100% health. I essentially became her **caregiver**. As the only child, anyone else taking care of my mother was not good enough for me, so I moved her in with us in Orlando. Unfortunately, this became one more strain on our marriage.

> **CAREGIVER** – a designated member of the family or a paid helper who takes care of the sick, elderly, or disabled.

The moment I knew it was a devastating hit to our marriage was when he voluntarily decided to move out of our bedroom to sleep in our daughter's room so that my mom could sleep in the room with me. He didn't verbally say anything offensive, and he was very empathetic with my mom. They got along well, but his demeanor instantly changed. While in Orlando, my mom's case was taken on by the Mayo Clinic in Jacksonville after the doctors in Saint Petersburg were

PSEUDOTUMOR OF THE SALIVARY GLAND – a fake tumor that is benign (non-cancerous) in the salivary gland (spit gland). The pseudotumor produces abnormal cells that begin mostly in your parotid gland or inside your cheeks. These tumors impact your salivary gland's ability to make saliva and keeping your mouth moist. When a psuedotumor is present it causes the patient extreme pain in the area behind the ear and jaw area. Operative surgery called a glandular sialoadenectomy is required to remove the calcified saliva.

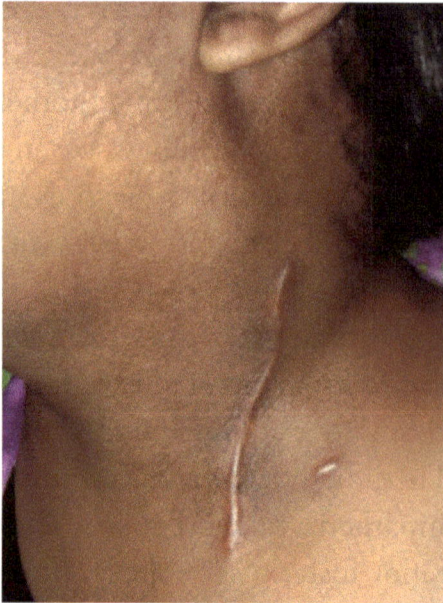

Mom's pseudotumor incision scar

unable to understand her condition. The doctors there were able to finally identify what was wrong. They found that she had a rare disease—a **pseudotumor of the salivary gland**. The thing about the pseudotumor was that though it was by definition a fake tumor, the body reacted like it was cancerous. We were told it was not a sickness normally seen in African

Americans but more common in Asian men. The next step was a very invasive surgery with a vertical incision on the left side of her neck. They took out all of the pseudotumor. We had recovery and relief, and my mother did eventually return to Saint Petersburg after getting so much better. However, I went back into a broken marriage and a husband who stopped coming home.

My husband had a lot of family in Orlando. He ended up staying at his aunt's house many nights because of the stress at our house, and that was the major demise of our marriage. For me, I was simply in survival mode and trying to give what I felt others needed, trying to make it work on all ends. I attempted to make it a group and global effort, but it had escaped me that everyone's needs were different. I thought of the conversations I would have with my dad, who wasn't the type to care if someone wasn't happy with your decision. I remembered him telling me, "*You're doing your best. If someone doesn't like it, f**k them.*" That was the kind of candor from a man that I was expecting. I felt that my husband at that time saw all the pressure I was going through and would understand if I wasn't stroking his ego, being attentive to his immigration issues, or having enough play dates with the baby. I thought that he knew I was doing the best that I could, but it didn't come across that way. Later on during my conversations with him, he revealed that he felt I was putting him last and that whenever we were anywhere together, he was never seen. He was always on the back burner for Kentaya. Whether with my career, my mother, or my education, he felt that I was this superwoman doing all these things and he couldn't do the same after that for me and for himself. To him, I was the one wearing the pants and navigating life better than him, but that didn't come out in communication, and it started to tear us apart. With regard to cheating, he attracted people and women who could fulfill the needs that he had. It was hard on me because I didn't understand his responses. I was unaware at that time that he was cheating. What I knew was that there was this negative energy he was projecting, and I didn't understand it because I was doing the best that I could. In my eyes, I thought he saw that and all I was doing for our family. I wasn't just doing it for his daughter or him, but for our family. I wondered why he didn't understand.

Eventually I discovered that he was cheating and in 2008, I decided we needed to figure out life separately. I planned to move out of our home so that our daughter wouldn't be put in a position where she would not have a home. I never wanted her to feel abandoned, but I knew at that point, I had to keep my sanity. He wasn't being grateful or respectful, and he was putting my life at risk by sleeping with women, increasing the chances of transmitting diseases to me. There was a woman who sent him a Father's Day card written in Spanish to our home, so I knew he was having sex with women and it was highly possible unprotected sex. On top of that, my health was suffering as I began to experience migraines and tension headaches again, thinking it was all related to stress. It took one conversation with myself to decide what stressors were necessary and unnecessary, and I decided that my marriage was an unnecessary one. I was added to the equation. I didn't have to be married, and I didn't have to be a stepmother, a decision he made even easier when he started leaving for long periods of time and decided to take our daughter with him so I wouldn't complain about being left alone with her. Did I just pack up and exit? No. I informed him that I was leaving. I packed my things and moved in with a business partner who lived 20 minutes from me.

Leaving my marriage was a horrible feeling. I felt terrible. I felt lost. I felt in a daze and at that point, unappreciated. I was a single, successful woman who made the decision to bring a man and his child into my home and change my life in an effort to properly raise his daughter. I married him and gave him the opportunity to do well with his education and career, and all he had to do was keep his focus on his family and complete his immigration paperwork. But he focused on his web of lies to try to hide his cheating. There wasn't anything else I could do for him or the family but to bow out gracefully. I could no longer put myself in that situation. In October of 2008, I finally began my transition. Moving out was a hell of a day. I made sure to do so before our daughter came home from school, and thank goodness I did because he went ballistic. He attempted to fight the movers as they were taking out my stuff. He was trying to snatch things out of their hands. What made everything even more crazy was that my preparation to move was a three-month process. I gave him notice, and I even began moving certain items into storage. I guess he was so caught up in what he was doing that he failed to notice the pieces of furniture, pictures, and dishes removed. He was also unemployed due to his immigration status. After that, he only stayed in the apartment for a few months and then he moved back to New York with our daughter.

In January, after the entire transition and then working full time at the school, I was still having significant headaches. One day while I was teaching my class, I began to stumble while lecturing. A piercing sound bounced around in my head, sounding like nails on the chalkboard. When I finally took a seat and regained my thoughts, I asked the students if they heard that screeching sound and everyone said no. I immediately released class and called my doctor and demanded an MRI, as the multiple visits to the emergency room where they took CT scans were not showing any issues. I knew this time it was really a problem. This felt different. Even the headaches I experienced while living in New York never felt like this. I remember the one time my head was hurting so bad I lost my eyesight for 10 minutes, pure darkness. But still, this head pain caused me to feel different, so I needed an MRI. When I received the results, the reality of my pain finally came to light. There in the campus gym I got the phone call that would change me forever. My doctor's voice was riddled with the kind of concern no patient wants to hear from the doctor calling them about

PITUITARY MACROADENOMAS are benign epithelial neoplasms composed of adenohypophyseal cells. Trust me, this sounded as weird to me then as it does now. Basically, it's not brain cancer but if left untreated, it can cause serious illness because it affects the normal pituitary gland, optic nerves, and the brain.

their results. I had a brain tumor. It was a **macroadenoma of the pituitary gland**. His words to me were, "*You needed to get to a neurosurgeon yesterday.*" I was immediately numb. I could hear him shouting *"Hello?"* on the other end, but I was disconnected from reality. When I reconnected to my body, I finally asked him what this all meant. He told me I needed to have surgery right away, especially because of the size of the tumor, or I could experience apoplexy. Apoplexy meant the tumor would burst and I would bleed from the inside out, which it was dangerously close to doing since it was at its maximum "macro" size. At any moment, that could happen in my brain. It was time to stop and make quick decisions like never before.

THE LESSON

Getting a divorce wasn't in my plans at all, as I believe is the case for many divorced couples. Nobody gets married with plans to get a divorce eventually. In fact, as a child of divorced parents, I didn't think it would be my situation because I thought I had seen and learned from my parents. My marriage was going to be different. But marriage comes with a lot of uncertainties, and you never see them going in. You find someone you love, believe that they are everything to you and nothing could ever go wrong, and then you decide to spend the rest of your life with them. At that stage, you're not seeing any red flags. Whatever anyone says to you about them doesn't matter because all you see is love. I wouldn't say I wasn't thinking straight when I decided to start a family with my ex-husband. I was. I loved him and the child, and I don't regret jumping in to save her. I just wish he had actually seen my efforts and fought for us instead of cheating. One thing I have come to understand about marriage is that the moment one party stops fighting for the marriage to work, everything goes to shambles. I have realized that the two people in the relationship have to work together to make sure it works. It's not a one man or one woman thing.

I am no marriage counselor, but I would tell new couples that communication is key. In fact, it is important in all relationships, whether romantic, platonic, or business. Imagine having a business partner and not communicating your thoughts with them. The business is bound to fail. It's the same way with romantic relationships, too. I believe that there are some issues that would have been resolved in relationships and saved a lot of marriages if only people had communicated. Then there are those who think they are communicating but in the real sense, they're just having a monologue. You have to make sure the person you're communicating with understands you and responds. That's the only way communication works. Through proper communication, you can save your marriage if both of you think it's worth saving.

"I WILL ALWAYS COMMUNICATE WITH THE PARTIES INVOLVED IN ANY RELATIONSHIP I FIND MYSELF IN, AND IF IT DOESN'T WORK, I WILL UNDERSTAND THAT I PUT IN MY BEST EFFORT."

TABLETOP 5

SAVING ME FROM MYSELF

THE STORY

*"In that moment, I understood what was important:
Life was worth living. I impacted the lives of others,
and my life was also worthy." ~ Dr. Kentaya Beeler*

Telling my mom about my doctor's report was the
last thing I wanted to do. She immediately goes into
panic mode whenever she gets bad news. She drove from
Saint Petersburg to Orlando to be with me as I took a few
days off from work to put a plan into motion. I was told that
I needed a second opinion, so that is what I sought. The first
appointment I made was at Shands Hospital in Gainesville,
and the second was at a neurology clinic in Saint Petersburg,
where my mom knew a few neurosurgeons. Between those
days, I was on an emotional rollercoaster. Some days I felt
fine, and it gave me hope that the doctor's original report was
incorrect. On other days, I was hit with episodes of dizziness
and every word the doctors told me would replant in my spirit.
It became very scary for me, especially when I started to trip

over myself. It was almost as if the tumor was slowly taking over the body that was once mine. Despite the warnings from my body and the urgency from the neurosurgeons, I pushed the surgery off in hopes of receiving two or three more opinions that I prayed would be in my favor. However, every day that I prolonged the surgery meant a greater chance for the tumor to burst. If that occurred, it would bleed into my brain, eyes, and even mouth. The journey to get other opinions was very aggravating, to say the least. To go to the

---

```
PATIENT NAME:  BEELER, KENTAYA

ADMISSION DATE:  06/02/2009
DISCHARGE DATE:

DATE OF BIRTH:  10/12/1977
OPERATIVE REPORT


DATE:   06/02/09

PREOPERATIVE DIAGNOSIS:  Pituitary adenoma.

POSTOPERATIVE DIAGNOSIS:  Pituitary adenoma.

NAME OF OPERATION:  Left endonasal transsphenoidal resection of
pituitary adenoma.



ANESTHESIA:  General.

COMPLICATIONS:  None.

BLOOD LOSS:  Negligible.

HISTORY:  This is a 31-year-old woman with a pituitary adenoma that
has progressively enlarged.  It is nonsecretory.  Because of
progressive enlargement, decision was made to pursue surgical
intervention.  The risks of procedure including bleeding, infection,
spinal fluid leak, meningitis, damage to the carotid arteries causing
massive hemorrhage and/or stroke and death, panhypopituitarism
requiring hormonal supplementation, optic nerve damage causing visual
loss and/or permanent blindness, were all disclosed.  Patient
understood her risks, benefits and alternative treatment options, and
her radiographic studies, and she agreed to pursue surgical
intervention.
```

Dr. Beeler's Brain Surgery Risk Report

neurology offices and hear them tell me they were backed up for six weeks was very stressful. There was a clear message of lack of empathy, despite my vulnerability and the delicacy of my situation. These people who worked in these offices saw me as just another brain tumor case because it was their everyday norm. Unfortunately, the treatment I received at my job did not bring any needed relief. I was working as a full-time professor and my schedule was packed with classes. The college was pestering me about who would cover my classes while I was out. I utilized the HIPAA regulations to my advantage and refused to disclose my health concerns to them. However, it only added unneeded stress to my struggles finding a qualified neurologist because setting up appointments that did not conflict with my lecture schedule seemed like an unattainable task. On one hand, time was not on my side, and I needed an appointment as soon as possible. On the other hand, I needed to maintain my job and not miss a lot of lectures as that would impact my students' learning and alarm my employer that my health condition was dire, which could affect continued employment. This is key when you are employed in an At-Will state like Florida, where an employer can release you of your duties without a reason or warning. In addition, having good insurance benefits was also a concern when my employment was at risk. For me, the college covered my medical insurance 100% but I was limited to the neurosurgeon in my healthcare network.

Finally, I was sent to a medical practice where there was only one neurosurgeon in the network for the college's insurance policy. After that, I did my research on the neurosurgeon, who had one judgment against him but it was resolved and settled. All his other ratings were very good. Even the other two neurosurgeons I met with informed me that he was one of the best. After I met with him, I made the decision to go into surgery on June 2, 2009. From that appointment, everything was like a time race. Every day I woke up, I didn't know how I was going to feel or if I could focus. Even my visual ability started to be impacted. It was clear that I really was sick, even though there were days I felt perfect. That was stressful. The most soul-shaking experience, the cherry on top of this entire ordeal, was when I told my husband what was going on. I was in a tight situation, especially when it came to timing. My mother was my main support, but she was already booked to take a cruise two weeks after my surgery. Not wanting to be a burden for my mother, I told her that I still wanted her to go on the trip. She agreed that she would not miss it and decided to reach out to my husband, who moved back to New York with his mother, to ask if he would come to Florida and stay with me for the one week that she would be on her cruise. When talking to my mother, you would have thought he was someone I could count on because after all, we were there for each other in other challenging times like my knee surgery and stepping in during our daughter's neglect. When my mother contacted him to see if he would be available to stay with me for that week, he said *"Okay."* He would see what he could do.

During the few weeks before my surgery, there was so much paperwork to review and prepare. It was during that time I was introduced to end-of-life preparations. Forms like Do

SPOUSAL RIGHTS REGARDING ADVANCED DIRECTIVES – An advanced directive is legally recognized but not legally binding. Therefore, in a medical emergency healthcare providers may seek end of life decisions from the next of kin and in a marriage, the spouse is considered the next of kin. Regardless of written advanced directives, the spousal decision can supersede if present when the medical crisis occurs.

Not Resuscitate (DNR), wills, living wills, and appointing a healthcare surrogate were overwhelming but critical to the brain tumor removal procedure. After meeting with an attorney, I was informed of **spousal rights in end-of-life decisions**. This jaded me because, although my husband and I were separated, I was reluctant to divorce him because of his immigration status. I knew divorcing him would ruin his chances at successfully reinstating his residency in the United States. Although he had done me dirty, divorcing him would impact our daughter's life with the one biological parent she solely depended on. So yes, I was willing to let him live his life married to me although we were not together UNTIL, and I mean *UNTIL*, the attorney told me if I should have life-threatening or altering effects from my brain surgery, my husband would automatically have primary decision-making authority over my body. He could enforce or disregard my **advanced directives** that I had

Advanced Directives

written in my living will and my DNR decision. It was at that point I knew a divorce was imminent and my first priority before the brain surgery. So I immediately informed him and he agreed. We filed for dissolution of marriage and our divorce was finalized January 21, 2009. Even after the divorce, he was the one who still wanted us to be a family. I made sure my mother was listed as my caregiver in the event anything happened to me, not him. Would he really be there for me when I needed him the most?

I remember going out to Walmart, buying the brightest scarf, and writing with a permanent marker, *"God is able!"* It

Dr. Beeler with her parents on the day of surgery.

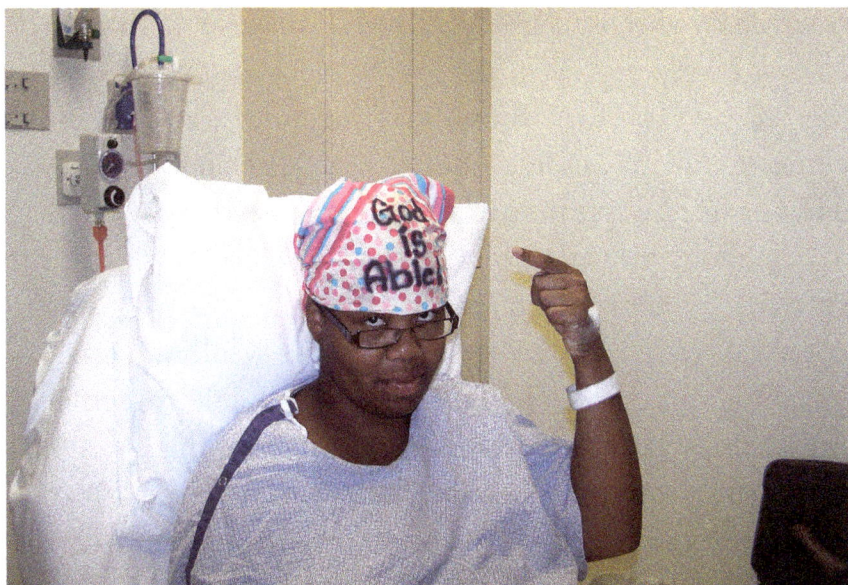

Dr. Beeler Prepped For Surgery

was at that moment that I agreed to write a will. I agreed to sign the paper with the neurosurgeon, acknowledging that I accepted the risk of fatality. I accepted the risk of stroke and not being who I was before. It was nerve-wracking, but I understood that it was God's divine wisdom that was going to operate in that room. It was God's divine ability that would wake me up and restore me to who I was. There wasn't anything in medical science that could give me a promise. That was written on the preoperative risk report. It was the word of the doctors, and I had to agree to it. A couple of nights before my surgery, I called my ex-husband to go over the last few details before his arrival to help me after my surgery. On the phone with him, the most despicable thing came out of his mouth: *"Do you really think I'm going to* come down there after you left me? Remember you could do bad all by yourself? Well, now you're doing it. I'm not coming. You tell your mama." Those were his words, and he didn't come. I told my mom, riddled with disbelief. I was hurt and felt like he spit in my face. My mom didn't say any bad words about him not coming but in true mom form, she created an emergency plan and got some of my cousins to come out to help me. They took shifts. While she was still unsure about going on the cruise, I was able to convince my mom that it was something I truly didn't want her to miss. I wanted her to have that time off as a caregiver. Despite having that emergency plan, I was still stressed and my ex-husband's response was a real hit to the gut. At that point, I didn't even think that it would be a bad thing if I were to die. I remember talking to God and telling Him that if I died while under anesthesia, it would be okay. The one thing that shifted the atmosphere was the arrival of my dad. Despite the fact that our relationship was now strained after the years of disappointment, he showed up that day at the hospital. I remember my dad wrapping his arms around me and laying hands on me to pray.

There in his arms he said to me, *"I love you. You are the epitome of a fighter. We named you Kentaya after Kunta Kinte. We thought you were a boy, and you came out a girl, and you have done everything at this point to be more powerful than if a man had a son in his arms."* While continuing to lay in his arms, he was pouring out his heart to me. He continued, *"I know you are going to beat this because you have the fight in you. Ever since you were born a premature baby and had to fight to come home out of the NICU, you have been a fighter baby, and I love you. If there is anything that I have ever done to make you feel abandoned, I apologize for that."* Those were his words. My heart was never so overwhelmed. He finished by telling me we were going to fight through this, get on the other side, and we would win this together. For the first time in a long time, I didn't feel as if he had failed me. I didn't feel abandoned by him or that he was only there for me for his own personal gain, as all men had been to me. Those nuggets of wisdom and being surrounded by people who had such hope in their eyes, not knowing the thoughts of death swarming my mind, was refreshing. That changed the trajectory right there in the pre-operating room.

Knowing that and experiencing my ex-husband turn his back on me after I was there for him and his child in need made it hurt less. All that hurt did not matter in that room with my mom, dad, and cousin. In that moment, I understood what was important: Life was worth living. I impacted the lives of others, and my life was also worthy. I loved myself enough that I felt like I had more living to do.

Going down that hallway to the operating room with my family and my dad leading, I heard him say to the operating room staff, *"This is precious cargo."* He was very emotional, and I remember my mom trying to calm him. Dad was a crier, so tears were falling like a waterfall from his eyes, although he was trying to hold them back while holding on to the rails of the gurney. The moment we got to the point of no return, when my family could no longer walk with me, the nerves started to settle back in. There in the room, they went over the different equipment they were going to use. My doctor came in to give me a pep talk and from there, it was time. As they injected fluid in me, I could feel my body going to sleep. I set my mind on Him, God, who was in control, and whispered, *"Okay God, it's just You and me now. It's going to be what it's going to be. Either I'm coming home with you or I'm coming back."* I was scared just saying that, but I said it anyway, and then I went to sleep!

When I woke up, I was groggy but alert enough to hear them call my name and hear them say, *"She's alert! She's alert!"* I remember that I was in, I guess, the ICU. When I came to full cognitive awareness, I remember being in excruciating pain but yet still sitting straight up. I gazed outside the window to gain a sense of where exactly I was. As soon as my mouth and my brain could connect with each other, I shouted for my mother. The nurses promptly came to my aid, telling me that my family was near but left to get something to eat. I laid back down, thriving in pain, begging for relief. The nurse gave me some pain killers, but then said to me *"We can't give you much because you have pain med allergies."* She said to me *"You are allergic to codeine, percocet, and demerol, and all medicines in that family, so I can only give you this."* My dad and I have this in common. We have allergies to specific meds. My allergies to pain medications were discovered when I had impacted wisdom teeth removed during my college years. Taking codeine, percocet, and demerol caused my blood pressure to drop and removed my ability to blink my eyes. That resulted in the ambulance being called and the hospital pumping my

Do you know your medical allergies?

I Keep It All
Together Project

stomach and my veins being flushed with saline after seven sticks to relieve me from coding. It was there the ER physician said, *"Young lady, never take any of these meds again. It may be fatal."* That friendly reminder humbled me, and I laid there waiting for my family.

After they returned, I remember fussing at them about leaving me, which of course they explained that they had been there since the time they brought me out. They said that they had briefly left to get something to eat. When night time came, my father and cousin left because only one person could stay with me. There in the night, my sodium dropped very low due to the high levels of water I consumed before the surgery. That, combined with my not eating due to the fact that I was sleepy from the anesthesia, caused my sodium to drop. Low sodium in brain surgery patients can lead to lasting brain damage or fatalities. I don't know what they did, but they were able to bring up my sodium. The next morning, shockingly, the doctor ordered me to be discharged. That would be when all the drama started.

THE LESSON

Have you ever gone through a painful experience and felt like that was the most horrible thing that would ever happen to you in your life, but then you experience another pain that supersedes the one you felt previously? I think the first hurt I experienced was when my parents got divorced. I felt hurt and betrayed when it happened, especially when my dad started a new family. Then, when I lost my grandmother and experienced breaking up with my high school love, I thought that was the last time I would be that hurt. But life kept throwing a lot at me. It is only through God that I'm able to stay strong. I don't think when God made us, He expected us to go through things alone. This is why I mentioned having a good circle of family and friends and a support system while trusting God to help you survive whatever life throws at you. If you decide to do life alone, you will be drained. Seeing my dad and my family around me before my surgery gave me hope that everything would be okay, and no matter the outcome, I had a family that loved me. Would I have loved it if my ex-husband showed up? Yes! But his not showing up made me understand how real seasonal love is!

If I could talk to my younger self, I would tell her that she would experience a lot of pain and hurt in her life. She would be betrayed by people, experience pain from sickness, and find herself in life or death situations, but she should stay positive and strong through it all. Wait, maybe I don't have to tell my younger self that because it's a part of life's journey. Despite everything I've been through, I have always tried to remain positive and strong. It is always hard to see a different side to whatever you're going through, but somehow I managed to. I knew that there were two options for me when I went into surgery. Either I survived and returned to my family and life, or I died and went home to rest. I was okay with either option because it felt like a win-win to me. Life won't always go as planned, but staying positive will help you survive. Well, that was what my banking rep told me when he applauded me for taking out **disability insurance** on my car loan. It's funny how believers of Christ can be strategically placed during life decisions. That insurance came into effect when I was out because of my brain surgery.

CREDIT DISABILITY INSURANCE is a financial product that many banks offer loan borrowers. Borrowers who experience an illness or injury causing them not to work can take advantage of the insurance benefit, which makes their loan payments until they return to work.

I have also realized that the energy around you when you're going through bad things matters a lot. If the people around you are negative or have some level of hatred toward you, it impacts your energy too and may determine the outcome of your experience. If my family would have had bad energy or were not motivating and strong through my surgery experience,

I'm not sure I would have had a positive mindset going into the operating room. That's why it is important that you surround yourself with people who actually love you, pour into you, and have positive energy. You know those faith walkers!

"WHEN LIFE THROWS ME A CURVEBALL, I WILL LEAN INTO THE PITCH WITH POSITIVE ENERGY."

GLUE 6

HEALING IS MORE THAN PHYSICAL

THE STORY

"I wanted to go to sleep and just die peacefully, but I found myself waking up every morning. It felt like God was intentionally messing with me because I didn't understand why He would wake me up to so much pain and suffering." ~ Dr. Kentaya Beeler

THERE IN THE BATHROOM, THE DOCTOR AND I STOOD. IN my nostril laid a thick material looking like a maxi pad that went all the way back to my brain. The white string dangled out, and the doctor slowly pulled it to bring the entire pad out. *"Open your mouth and yawn,"* were the instructions he gave me. When I did, I could feel the pad all the way from the back of my neck to my lips. My doctor pulled the string, and I felt everything in my head hurt. It was almost like I was puking, but I couldn't gag. When he was done, he looked at me and said, *"Okay, you can go home."* I was so confused, and I was still disoriented. When I asked for an explanation, it came down to the simple issue of payment. By me staying,

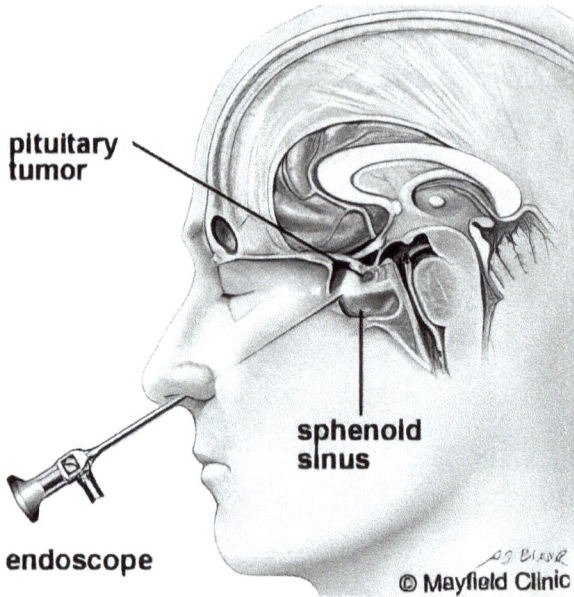

pituitary
tumor

sphenoid
sinus

endoscope

© Mayfield Clinic

TRANSPHENOIDAL BRAIN SURGERY is a procedure that involves accessing the base of the skull through the nose, usually to remove a tumor of or near the pituitary gland. The surgeon passes instruments through the nose and cuts the bone underneath the brain to reach the tumor.

they would tell the insurance company that I was choosing to stay and the result of that would be the insurance company not paying. This started the process of me going from bad to worse. I checked into a timeshare in Orlando that was cleaned thoroughly because I was very susceptible to sickness due to

---

*   (n.d.). Endoscopic pituitary surgery (transsphenoidal). Mayfield Brain and Spine. https://mayfieldclinic.com/pe-endopitsurg.htm

the type of brain procedure I had undergone. It was called **transphenoidal brain surgery**. With my sinus cavity open, I was at high risk of infection.

Over the weekend, I was in excruciating pain as my head was hurting but it was a different type of hurt than the headaches before surgery. I also noticed that I couldn't keep my balance. I couldn't walk without assistance to go to the restroom. In addition, when I tried to sit up in bed, the room would spin. It was my mother who noticed the difference in my overall health. When she called the surgeon's office, the nurse explained that some people have an adverse reaction to the anesthesia. My mother explained to them that I never had an issue with or a reaction to anesthesia prior. The nurse proceeded to tell her that it was OK and that they would schedule me for an appointment on Monday. That was five days after I'd had the surgery. The nurses were adamant that it was not abnormal for a person to feel weakness in their lower extremities and be lightheaded. The rest of the weekend, I pretty much had the same issues where I wasn't able to focus or walk. I was told to stay away from cell phones, so all technology was being run by my cousin. I was pretty much just left alone to rest.

Because of my allergies to pain killers, I was only given flexeril. I did take some vicodin but it was too strong for me and I couldn't take any of the stronger medicine that they would normally give patients like percocet or demerol, so I was in excruciating pain. If you've ever seen those movies where people are watching the clock, that was how I felt. I was doing that whenever I wasn't asleep because of the pain. I always looked forward to daybreak. Fast forward to Monday.

When we went to the doctor. I was unable to keep my balance, so I used my mom's shoulders for support. My cousin put her hand on my back, and I was really struggling to walk. When I got to the doctor's office, the nurse said, *"Well, what's going on here?"* because I looked sick and there were other patients there for consultations. My mother told them about how I was still having trouble walking, so they rushed me back into a room and said that was better because I was scaring other patients. My mom told them that it wasn't our intention to scare anyone but to inform them about what was going on with me. Nobody said I was going to experience this. In fact, they said I would be able to return to work two weeks after the surgery, so why was I having trouble walking? The doctor came into the room and asked what was going on. My mom was about to explain, but he cut her short and said I should explain it instead. I told him that I had trouble controlling my legs, and then he told me to stand up and asked several questions. He said the issue did not come from the part of the brain that he worked on and that they've never had anyone with the inability to walk after surgery, so there was probably something else wrong with me. I asked him what it was then because I could walk well before the surgery and ever since the surgery, I hadn't been able to regain that function. He said he wasn't going to go back and forth with me because whatever I had going on wasn't their fault, and they knew nothing about it. I told him that I wasn't saying that they did anything wrong. What I was trying to tell them was that I had issues moving my leg, and it wasn't because I didn't have the will to do it. I just couldn't. He ordered the nurse to get me on physical therapy and said he was going to release me back to work.

My experience with the doctor felt different from the person that I consulted with before my surgery. He suddenly didn't care anymore and kept repeating the fact that he had done his job and what I was going through wasn't his fault. They told me to go get a cane from Walgreens or another store so I would stop leaning on my mom. I was totally dismissed, and I felt very rejected. I was straight up lost. I was happy that I survived the surgery, but I was confused that they sent me home when I couldn't walk. In fact, I began to think they intentionally sent me home the next day after brain surgery because they knew I was going to have complications and they didn't want to be held responsible. Something had to have gone wrong in the surgery because being sent home the next day after surgery when the insurance company pre-authorized a three-day stay in the hospital wasn't making any sense.

My employer, on the other hand, was already checking to see when I was going to resume work. They didn't know the details of my surgery because of HIPAA requirements, but they knew that I had a major surgery. They needed to know when I would be back because the substitute was only supposed to replace me for two weeks. I told them I was having some post-op issues, and I didn't think I would make it back to work the following week. But the letter from my doctor said I was fit to resume work, so that left me in a dilemma. I had nothing to prove that I really couldn't walk and couldn't get back to my life as it was before surgery. I couldn't divulge the full details of my issues to the school because I didn't want to

SHORT-TERM DISABILITY INSURANCE is an insurance product that is used as supplemental income to be paid when an employee is temporarily out of work for three to six months due to a qualified medical condition such as after surgery rehabilitation.

scare them and also because I had the right not to. I asked if they could give me some more time for therapy. They said I had to fill out some paperwork for **short-term disability**, but my doctor still insisted he felt I could get back to work all in the name of still covering himself, so I had to go through my primary care doctor. That doctor and my endocrine doctor came together and decided that I did need the time off and filled out my paperwork, which gave me an extension to figure out what was wrong with me. My classes were covered for the rest of the summer. I went back to work in August because I had completed my short-term disability time off, which was just for 90 days, and there was no way to justify a long-term disability.

When I got back to work, everyone wanted to know what had happened to me. I told them that I had gait (walking) abnormalities, and many of them tried to research it. I don't know how it happened, but somehow a rumor spread around the college that I had brain cancer. My colleagues came to me asking why I didn't tell them that I had brain surgery. I wasn't exactly sure what to tell them or how to explain why I wasn't walking properly anymore because hell, I didn't even know myself. So, I just agreed with them that I had a brain surgery and that the doctors were not sure why I couldn't walk, and I had to take the summer off for them to figure it out. I don't know what reaction I was expecting from them, but I was surprised when they showed that they had a problem with me having brain surgery. They asked me to tell them more about the surgery because they felt it was a hazard for me to work on campus. Eventually, the school said I could no longer be a full-time professor, but they would allow me to continue to work as an adjunct lecturer. Since the time of my surgery, a Ph.D. was required to teach full-time in the program, and I only had a master's degree. They stated they were phasing out my position so I wouldn't continue to get any employee health benefits and my salary would be reduced by 60%.

I was bewildered by this news. It was completely strange that they were eliminating my position. Why did it have to be just my position, and why was it at that time? There was no one else in the department experiencing the phasing out, just me. I figured that they just wanted to get rid of me. I felt their unease when they questioned me about the details of my surgery. So, I went to the union and EEOC and asked if the college actually had the right to treat me that way. They said they could because Florida is an At-Will state but actually, they were not really letting me go because they didn't have a justification to do so. Instead, they were taking my full-time position and placing me in a part-time role. After discussing with my supervisor, the conclusion from the EEOC was that instead of teaching five classes, I could take 10 to make up for the salary reduction and be able to pay for my own benefits.

This seemed unfair to me because as a full-time employee, I was teaching five classes and earning well. I would have to teach double and still earn very little. I would work harder and still struggle to pay my health insurance, as my cobra coverage was $600 a month. Yes, I was going from free health insurance to $600 a month.

I remember the HR department calling and saying they heard that I had a problem with their counter-offer, and I explained how I thought it was inhumane. I was expected to work harder while walking on a cane and teach more than the number of classes I taught when I was a full-time professor for much lower pay. The HR rep said, *"You know, you don't have to work here. You have a choice."* I have experienced so much hurt in my life, but I think that hit deeper. I cried a lot because I had worked in the college for years. I was a part of a girls' mentorship program, and I worked in two departments. I loved my job so much and was so passionate about it. I left corporate accounting for it. All these things happened to me at a time when I really needed full benefits, full medical treatment, and a house. It felt like the world had turned against me, and I was all alone.

My ex-husband had left me with some unsettled bills, so I contacted him to tell him what I was experiencing and to see if he could pay his share of the outstanding bills because I got paid less during the summer as a result of the short-term disability leave I requested. I was trying to pick up the pieces. I also wanted to talk to our daughter because I did survive and I missed her. He told me again that I said I could do bad by myself, and I left him, so I should just do it myself. But he agreed he would let me talk to the baby. Silly me again, thinking there was an ounce of empathy in that man. It was like a yo-yo affect. Sometimes he would check in to see how I was feeling and have small talk and then it never failed, that cold side would prevail. At that moment, I went crazy because I wasn't begging him for money or asking for a favor. I was telling him to pay his own share of the bills that accumulated when we were together. I tried to explain my condition to him, especially my situation with the college, but he seemed uninterested and wasn't going to do the right thing. His insensitive reaction made me remember that there are people, especially men, who will just stick with you for a season as long as it can benefit them and when you need them, they disappear. I really needed some empathy from him or a reciprocation of the love I showed him when he was struggling, but there was nothing. He seemed so cold, and it made me wonder if the love I thought we shared initially was real.

I was struggling financially. Most colleges recruit in March or April, the latest in June, but there I was in December with a shaky job. I wasn't even physically fit to attend interviews as I was still using a cane. I did teach 10 — in fact, 12 — classes from January to April 2010. I also worked as an adjunct at night at two other schools. People thought I was a hustler and was brave, but it was a struggle to pay my bills. I bought a brace for my ankle so people would think that I only had a sprain and wasn't a liability. I was burnt out and mentally exhausted from that teaching load. I was still going to physical therapy, and they still couldn't figure out what was wrong with me. At some point, they said I would need to get a peg leg or shoes used for leg alignment. I told them that there was nothing wrong with my alignment. It all started after the surgery. I only got six weeks of visits to the physical therapist, so I was cut off when I exhausted my time. I also couldn't see doctors anymore because I couldn't afford the co-pays. I still had rent and my car payments. The endocrinologist who I thought was advocating for me was one of the doctors who cut me off when I could no longer make my co-pays, although I had an endocrine brain tumor. As time went by, it felt like I was losing everything. I lost my savings, but I was able to keep my apartment and my car. I knew I needed to find a way to start working from home because when people didn't see me, they didn't feel like I was a liability. In May 2010, when it dawned on me that I couldn't keep up with teaching 12 classes, I enrolled in a Ph.D. program. I told myself that I wasn't going to be tossed back and forth because I didn't have all the credentials I needed. I told myself that I am smart and that nothing should stop me from being the best. So obtaining a Ph.D. was a new milestone for me. I couldn't walk without an apparatus for 18 months until 2011, so pursuing a Ph.D. allowed me to stay home and receive financial aid benefits to supplement my income.

I prayed many nights that God would take me in my sleep because sometimes I just wanted to give up. I didn't want to do anything tragic, so I prayed every night that God would just take me out of my misery in my sleep. I wanted to go to sleep and just die peacefully, but I found myself waking up every morning. It felt like God was intentionally messing with me because I didn't understand why He would wake me up to so much pain and suffering. I soon realized that my Ph.D. program was giving me purpose. The topic I was working on was long-term care, and I

Dr. Beeler receiving electroencephalography therapy for balance issues after Brain Surgery

ELECTROENCEPHALOGRAPHY measures the electrical activity of the brain by using music and recording devices by applying electrode devices to the scalp. Patients with brain tumors, epilepsy, and sleep disorders are normally the population that has shown the most benefit from the testing.

enjoyed it so much. I started growing in my program and reading more about ways to protect your finances when you're hit with the unexpected. I found purpose as it was an opportunity to teach others how to prepare themselves for unforeseen circumstances. You don't necessarily have to be doing anything wrong to be caught in a situation like mine.

Although I was studying for my Ph.D. and that was giving me more of a positive mindset, my support system also helped me a lot. One of my friends was a DJ and he would invite me out to the club, as he knew music was therapeutic for me. He knew my neurologist was trying a new type of therapy using music called **electroencephalography**. He would say, *"Just come friend,*

Dr Beeler receiving aquatic core and balance therapy

come and sit in the corner and listen to the music. You have to get out of the house." My other friends knew that one of the therapeutic exercises was riding a swimming noodle in therapy. I would go to their apartment complexes and they would be my therapist as they watched me ride the noodle! That exercise strengthened my core and helped me with my balance issues. It was having those types of people around who would encourage me to keep going. I remember my friends convincing me to attend the Essence Music Festival, although I was still walking with a cane. I had decided that I needed to live my life because the diagnosis stated that I may never walk again without assistance since no one could explain my inability to walk on my own. In medical science, my experience was not a normal reaction to surgery. Only God could heal me to regain my walking ability. When visiting doctors to gain second and third opinions about my disability, there was one common message from them all. The doctors were saying *"At least you are alive. There are a lot of people who do not live through surgeries like yours."* My surgery had a 4% survival rate, and that fact changed my mindset.

Unfortunately, it took a while for things to turn around. It was a daily struggle to stay motivated because of what I was going through. It was almost two years later that I was laying in the bed and I had to go to the bathroom. I jumped up and it was just your normal go to the bathroom in the middle of the night. It did not hit me until I got to the toilet that I didn't have to use the wall to reach the restroom. For two years, I needed to put my hands up against the wall to scale my way to the restroom but that night, I didn't. It might have been 2 a.m. when I turned around to wash my hands and went back toward the bed. I just hollered and started crying. I called my mother and said, *"I can walk. I just went to the bathroom by myself without any help. I didn't have to grab the wall. I can walk. It was like a turtle, but I can walk."* For a while, I was shuffling. You know when you see older people shuffle their legs while walking. I continued to push myself, whenever I went out to not use a cane. However, I still keep the cane in my car to this day. The doctors said they don't know what turned off to allow me to walk on my own again and they don't know what could possibly trigger it to turn back on, which could cause my walking issues to return. They warned me to walk but to keep a cane nearby.

THE LESSON

I can't begin to describe the pain I have felt in my life. The funny thing is that it has been emotional as well as physical. I prayed that God would just take me in my sleep so it would all end. I had begged the doctors to figure out what was wrong with me but discovered that I was wasting my time because I wasn't going to find an answer. I didn't even know how to explain what was wrong with me to people. It all felt surreal.

In church, they often talked about faith and how we had to believe that things would get better. I discovered the concept of having faith as little as a mustard seed because that's the true definition of faith. Faith is not what you see but what you believe and that faith, no matter how little, can change a lot of things. You can will your way into and out of many things, You can will your way into joy just like you can will your way into depression, and you can will your way into mediocrity just like you can will your way into winning. I willed myself into getting better. After seeing a little progress, I believed that I was going to be 100% better, even though it seemed impossible. I had even forgotten what it felt like to be able to walk properly. There was also no one to reassure me that I could be perfectly okay again, and that was a major teaching point for me. I had to learn the hard way that I don't need people to validate the things I believe. If God says it, that settles it. Your relationship with God should be personal. You don't need other people's validation or confirmation to believe His promises. When you realize this, you will notice a lot of changes in your life.

" I WILL ALWAYS PREPARE FOR UNFORESEEN CIRCUMSTANCES, AND I WILL NOT LOSE MY FAITH NO MATTER THE CIRCUMSTANCE. "

NAILED 7

BECOMING DR. BEELER

THE STORY

"An opportunity was brought to me to start a new life, but was I ready for what I prayed for? I answered the question with, 'Of course, oh yes, I'm positive. I am a very adventurous person.'" ~ Dr. Kentaya Beeler

I WAS GRADUALLY GETTING CLOSE TO MY PH.D. GRADUATION after having been in college for another six years. I started my doctoral program in 2010 and finished it in 2016. I was in the final chapters of my dissertation when my mentor retired. I was about to graduate, and a lot of people told me that they would give me a full-time job when I finished my doctorate. I was only working part-time so essentially, I had not worked a full-time job since 2012. I was finished with all my classes, and then my mentor needed to have back surgery so he retired. That launched me into a spiral backwards because the new mentor I started working with on my dissertation committee in 2015 disagreed with my study.

My work was based on the tax deduction for long-term care insurance, and it was a qualitative study. Most financial majors do quantitative studies because accounting is based on its numerical foundation, whereas qualitative is more about interviews and sitting down and getting a feel for lived experiences. My study was based on the experiences of self-employed individuals I interviewed to find out if they had heard of long-term care insurance and how it would impact their tax return. My new mentor was not happy with me pursuing a qualitative study and insisted that I conduct a quantitative study that would take statistical data, crunch it, and then make a different theory of it. He basically said, *"I'm not sure what your other mentor was doing, but I'm not signing off on this. I wouldn't agree with a qualitative study."*

Well at that point, you know me, the champion spirit ignited and I went back and forth in a rebuttal with the college. That took about three months, and I still had to pay per term even if I didn't get any work done. Then I was approaching the maximum threshold of financial aid because I had completed a bachelor's and a master's degree and I was in the fifth year of my Ph.D. I was told if I didn't finish the program within a couple months, I would not have any financial assistance. At that point, I didn't have money to pay for a Ph.D. program. I had to go through the Scientific Merit Review Board (SMRB) and explain why I felt like my study would address a gap in the body of knowledge. I finally received a go ahead from the board to only get notice that the new "pain in my side" mentor had been removed from the college because of a drug addiction. Then I was stuck with being assigned to another mentor who agreed that I should have a quantitative study. So I said, *"Oh no, we aren't doing this again!"* I went back and showed all who had approved my qualitative methodology approach and pulled documents going back to 2013. After proving that, they let me keep the topic and continue my dissertation from where it was, but the third mentor said he would not put his signature on my dissertation unless I added 75 pages. At that point, I was already up to like 200 typed pages and thought I was at the end of my writing.

"What do you mean add 75 pages? Insert them where?" He told me, *"It doesn't matter where you insert them. I need 75 more pages before I will even look at this and put my signature on it for you to graduate."* By that time, graduation had been approved for March 2016. The SMRB concluded that I could continue with my current study since I had 200 or more pages, so I could move forward with graduation. The dissertation would not be finished until I had a signature from the mentor who wanted the additional pages. This was indeed a dilemma. Having to add 75 pages meant I needed to go back and revise everything. He also said to take out the exhibits, including sample tax returns and all of the additional diagrams. He wanted pure pages with very small diagrams.

March 2016 was approaching quickly. I had sent out my graduation invitations and made plans to still show up in New Orleans, but my dissertation was not approved. I didn't stop advocating for academic remediation, instead I escalated my situation all the way up to the president of the School of Business. I told her, *"I don't walk across stages. I graduate."* I did not want to just walk at commencement. The president encouraged me to come to graduation, which was in March, and to bring my rebuttal packet to her. I eventually agreed because I would meet someone with authority in person. I was excited for commencement and then found out you're supposed to only get three tickets. Because so many people understood my struggle and wanted to be there, I needed an additional 26 tickets. I had a whole tribe. This was an achievement for them all, and guess who sent an RSVP? My daddy! This would be his first collegiate graduation. He wasn't there for my bachelor's or master's graduation, but was going to show up. I was very excited to have everybody there, but I was also disappointed because I felt like a fraud. Even though a lot of people walk across the stage when they've not really graduated, I have never been in that situation knowingly before. Graduation weekend in New Orleans was spectacular. We celebrated birthdays, ate beignets, took a pole-dancing class, completed an escape room adventure, and even had graduation-themed shirts! My worries escaped me but were there while at the pre-commencement dinner. The president and I met and to my surprise, she was a Black woman. She was very well put together, with silver hair, an immaculate silk press, and makeup laid to perfection. We spoke for some time, and she took the rebuttal packet. She told me that she would look at it. When I came back from graduation in April 2016, she said, *"Listen, I can't stop your mentor from asking you to get 75 more pages. Get 75 more pages, then let's talk again."* I was devastated.

I started working on the revisions in the heat of tax season. I couldn't dedicate 100% of my time but after April 15, I shut down any revenue-generating activities to complete the 75 pages. I camped out in the library to rewrite my dissertation and in May, I got a random email that said, *"Hi, I see that you're approaching getting a Ph.D. in accounting. Have you ever thought about working in the United Arab Emirates? If you are considering this opportunity, contact us."* I thought it was spam, so I deleted it. About a week later, while I was again studying at the library, I got another email saying, *"Hey, I reached out to you before. I am a recruiter for the governments of Dubai in the United Arab Emirates. We see that you are about to graduate."* I had posted my curriculum vitae online. *"We're looking for professors with your experience. Would you consider a job in the United Arab Emirates?"* I did respond back, saying, *"Is this real or is this spam?"* The person got right back to me and said, *"No, this is very real. We would like to set up our first interview with you on the phone in a week."* I went to that interview even though I was still studying and revising my dissertation. Amazingly, within two hours of getting off the phone, they said I had been shortlisted and would be moving up to a second interview. The officials from the government of the United Arab Emirates would be interviewing candidates in person in Seattle, Washington. I became excited and worried at the same time because I didn't have the money to travel to Seattle due to not generating income. I told them I was in Florida, and it was a bit of a distance for me to get to Seattle. They said they would pay for my plane ticket and my hotel stay. Then I said, *"What?"* That is how I knew it was real.

I flew out to Seattle, and I almost forgot about the stress of getting my dissertation done. I was feeling like I finished because I walked across the stage and these people were seeking me for a job. I was excited and a bit nervous when I walked into the room. There were a lot of people in business suits. I checked in at the front desk, and they told me what room to go to. I walked in with my business suit, pulling a look from my old FAMU college dress-up days and being a bank auditor. They told me to wait, and then they called me for the interview. There was a long conference table with Middle Eastern men surrounding the table, approximately 9 of them. They were not wearing the Ghutra, the cultural headwrap, but you could tell that they were Emirati and spoke Arabic. They had this dark stare. I was the only woman in the room and the only person of color by the hue of their skin, even though they had more of an olive tone. They had me sit at the head of the table with a laptop and a camera facing toward me. They told me that they were going to record the interview because, after the interview, they would go back to the United Arab Emirates and share it with their personnel. From there, they would make their hiring decision. The interview took about 30 minutes. They asked me a variety of questions about my experience, such as corporate accounting and teaching accounting. Then they asked if I had ever lived abroad. That was the first time I felt that I might not be a fit for the position because I had never lived overseas. They asked me if I would be bringing any family with me, and I said, *"No."* Then it hit me in the interview: *"I'm going essentially alone."* The fact that I no longer had a husband or a child allowed me to live in the experience of the interview and the great opportunity. But I was feeling nervous and a little bit condemned for not having a family. It could have just been the tone of the question, but I felt less accomplished at that moment.

They asked if I was sure that this was what I wanted to do. Although I had gotten on a plane from Tampa and went to Seattle, Washington, with no hesitation, it was at that moment that I thought, *"Was this really what I wanted to do?"* I had been praying for God to heal my body and open a door for me. It had been since 2009, and things had just been going downhill for seven years. An opportunity was brought to me to start a new life, but was I ready for what I prayed for? I answered the question with, *"Of course, oh yes, I'm positive. I am a very adventurous person. I would love to impact the world in the field of accounting."* One of the major draws for me going there was that Dubai, in the United Arab Emirates, would soon be implementing taxation on goods and services. They never had that before. My experience in taxation; owning my own tax business, KB financial services; and teaching tax and accounting was why they specifically needed me. I would help the government roll out a new demographic of leaders in their country who would be educated on taxation. I finished up the interview, and I went to shake their hands and say thank you. They said, *"We are not allowed to shake women's hands, so it is no disrespect. We understand that this is your culture, but we cannot shake your hand."* That was another moment that hit me. Was I really ready for this? I said, *"No disrespect. Thank you for your opportunity."* I went about my way with an internal childlike grin.

I walked out and remembered someone saying, *"If you go to Seattle, make sure you go to Pike Place Market."* I went to the hotel, changed, and caught a taxi to Pike Place Market where fishermen are known for throwing fish at shoppers. I caught one. It was the first moment that I felt like I could breathe in such a long time. I went back to the hotel for my things and headed to the airport. During my connecting flight from Seattle, I opened up my phone and saw I had received an email alert that I had an offer. I couldn't believe they wanted me for the job, and I had not even made it home. They wanted to speak with me about my salary and when I could come, and they wanted to do that in three days. The offer had benefits worth $102,000, which would be exempt from U.S. taxes. They would also provide an allowance for my housing, salary, and a plane ticket for travel. This was important to me because I only had 67 cents when I went to Tallahassee for a job in 2012 and before that, the most I had ever made was $60,000. At that moment, someone saw my value and what I could offer them. They offered me $102,000! They would also cover my transportation and any moving expenses to get to them. I was blown away. This didn't seem real. Then they asked for me to send over the conferral of my degree. It hit me like a ton of bricks. They also said, *"Please report to work on August 5, 2016."* It was May, and I still hadn't finished the 75 pages. I said I was still waiting for my dissertation to be signed off on, and they said they just needed to make sure that they had proof of the conferred degree.

Degrees are only conferred at the end of each month, so I needed to try to see if I could get mine done in June. I completed my first set of revisions, and my mentor sent it back with more changes. It was no longer a 75-page issue but rather about 100 revisions in words and adjectives. It seemed like a simple fix, but every time I submitted edits, I had to go through a couple of weeks of prep. I no longer had the opportunity to get my degree conferred in June. I had to wait until July. I had to get proof of the degree to my employer so that I could start work in August. I hired a reviewer, which I had never done before, just to assess my work. I submitted it the last week of June. They said there was not enough time to get it reviewed by the end of the month. I reached out to my committee and told them that I had a job opportunity and needed my degree conferred by July. The committee members said they would work as diligently as they could. I finally had my committee meeting in July, and my degree was conferred on July 31, 2016.

THE LESSON

As I said in the previous chapters, for every stage of one's life, there are bound to be some challenges or setbacks that will make you want to give up. But as the scriptures state, God will not let you be tempted beyond your ability, and for every challenge there is a way of escape so that you may be able to endure it. So, if at any point you're going through some challenges that you believe might be the end for you, just remember that it is something you can handle and you will only come out stronger. I never thought I was going to have any problem getting my Ph.D. because I had a great dissertation topic, a great plan, and an understanding mentor. Everything was going smoothly, until it wasn't. I never thought in my life that I would have to walk across the stage without my actual degree again, but somehow I was able to battle through, not just with my degree but with a great job that many people wanted so badly.

I will always tell people that you have to stand up for yourself and fight for what you want because no one else will, not even your family or best friends. It has to be you fighting for what you deserve. I never kept quiet at any point, and I think that helped me a lot. When I wasn't getting what I thought I deserved, I spoke up, especially to the higher authorities. I was never shy or pushed to the side. I'm not sure I would have graduated in 2016 at all if I had kept quiet and let everyone push me around. If you want to achieve your goals and at the right time, you can't be pushed around. Yes, there is a difference between achieving your goals and achieving them at the right time. I would have obtained my degree eventually, but it may have been too late. I could have lost myself on the journey to achieving it. So make plans, set goals, and make sure you achieve your goals at the right time. The right time can be relative, though. What might be the right time for one person might not be the right time for another. Just know you and do you!

Dr. Beeler and Mom

Dr. Beeler and Dad

Dr. Beeler and Parents

"I REFUSE TO BE PUSHED AROUND.
I WILL ALWAYS FIGHT FOR WHAT
I BELIEVE IN AND DESERVE!
I'LL ALWAYS BE
A CHAMPION OF MYSELF."

VARNISHED 8

THE LIFE OF LUXURY

THE STORY

*"Everything put in writing isn't always
clear." ~ Dr. Kentaya Beeler*

IT WAS TIME TO DISCUSS MY NEW JOB WITH MY FAMILY. My
mom thought I was having a midlife crisis and was absolutely
against my move to Dubai. My dad was absolutely for it and
talked about how he actually had an opportunity to work in
Saudi Arabia back in the day when he built golf courses and
they really needed his expertise. He decided not to go because
his employer at the time felt that my dad might be at risk
because he is Black, so he never took the opportunity. He said
he would have been open to going and was excited about me
doing what he couldn't do. There were a lot of preparations,
and I didn't know anyone living in Dubai until one day I
discussed the move with another friend who lived in Atlanta
but was originally from St. Petersburg. She told me about her
friend, a former coworker of hers who moved to Dubai to
teach. She connected us via Facebook and the young lady

provided me with a lot of information about what to do to prepare. I started selling everything, including my washer and dryer. I was posting everything on Facebook without telling everybody that I was moving to Dubai. I took the job offer and had my degree conferred. I was truly ready! People knew that something was happening, but they didn't understand what. Some days I was really excited, and then some days I was really nervous. The job in Dubai seemed God sent because as the date grew closer for me to depart, I did not receive any job offers from the companies that I applied to in the U.S. God had already aligned me with the perfect job opportunity, I just knew it. It was nerve-wracking for me because a lot of people were saying things like, *"You're going to go by yourself? You just got over being sick not too long ago, and you are going to a foreign country that you know nothing about. You don't know anyone there. I thought that you were someone who makes sound decisions."*

I was all about stepping out in faith, and I needed a new start. The day before I was to leave, my mom was pleading with me. She kept on, saying, *"It's okay to change your mind."* I remember the young lady from Facebook telling me the biggest thing was to just get on the plane. If I got on the plane, I was going to be okay. I left Tampa airport on August 2, three days after my degree was conferred. My flight was scheduled for 6 a.m. My mother and three of my friends accompanied me to the airport. I had four huge suitcases because the young lady I had spoken to told me that there was a lack of our hair products over there. So, I had my hair stylist make me three custom wig units. I had all of my underwear because I was told that a lot of the clothing was Asian cut, so if it said extra large, it was probably a medium. With my physique, I decided to bring a lot of clothes. A big misperception is what clothes are socially acceptable in the culture. *"You can bring shorts, bathing suits, and dresses because it's hot,"* my online friend advised. I thought that we couldn't show our skin, but you can as long as you are respectful. My employer in Dubai kept saying there was going to be heat unlike what I had experienced before.

I got to the airport. We prayed there before I journeyed to the gate, and we took a picture. My mom did not want to take any pictures. She was never a picture taker and definitely not then. One of my friends was crying. The other one was kind of worried, but my mom was in shock. She still couldn't believe that I was really going. I was up the escalator and looking back, and I kept hearing my friend say, *"This will be the best decision of your life. Just get on the airplane."* I got through the checkpoints, and I became really nervous. My stomach was hurting, and I was thinking, *"What am I doing?"* All the negative things that people had been telling me started to weigh on me, but I was already there. My bags were already checked in, so I sat there until they told me to board. I got on the plane, and I was crying a lot. I wasn't loud, but I was sobbing. I couldn't stop the tears. It was the fear of the unknown. I was thinking, *"Really, Kentaya, you just recently started walking on your own and had a brain tumor. What are you doing?"* My body was in "go mode," and I just wanted to leave America. I called my mom to let her know that I had gotten on the plane, and she was very short with me. Then I called my dad, and he was really excited. He said it was going to be alright. Lastly, he said, *"What did your mom say?"* I told him that she wasn't happy. He told me that it was okay, and I had to remember that I had to live for myself. I had a connection in New York, and for the two-hour flight, I slept. I had cried myself to sleep. I got to JFK airport in New York and had a three-hour layover. I got something to eat because I knew that I was going to have a 12-hour flight from New York to Dubai. While there, I called my family in New York and told them that I was headed to Dubai. It was strange being in their town and not being able to see them. My aunt who I used to live with in New York prayed for my trip.

I flew JetBlue from Tampa to JFK. This was the first time I ever heard about the airline I used to get to Dubai. It was Emirates Airlines, for the actual United Arab Emirates. Once I stepped on the plane, I almost said, *"What the hell is this?"* It was as though I had stepped from the projects to the palace. The young lady who helped me prepare for my trip messaged me, and I told her that the plane was luxurious. There were royal purple and tangerine pillows on the seat. There was a beautiful aroma that filled the cabin. The stewardesses had on hats with long scarves and boasted red lipstick. All of their hair was neatly bunned. Their uniforms were strategically perfect, and when I came aboard, everyone welcomed me. This gave me a sense of peace when I first got on the plane. I wondered if this was a taste of the life that the young lady wanted me to see.

I sat down on the seat console, and there was a wide monitor in front of me. It was the widest monitor I had ever seen on a plane. I was told to bring my own pair of good headphones,

110

Dr. Beeler living in Dubai.

which I did. They had more than 1,000 movies and a lot of music channels. I was still in awe because I didn't know that this luxury existed. They provided me with a blanket and many other items for the flight. They made a welcome announcement that reminded me I had a 12-hour commute. All my fears hit me again, and my stomach bottomed out. I was like, *"Oh my God, I'm about to fly for 12 hours straight to where?"* I didn't know anything about where I was going. I got scared and started to cry again. I called my mom to let her know I was leaving, but she was still short and just said, *"Twelve hours, oh my God, that's crazy."* Then I called my dad, and he said, *"Twelve hours. How much gas do they got in there?"* He said it was going to be alright and asked if he had to wait 12

111

> **MEDICAL NOTE:**
> Understand the cost of transporting sick or deceased persons back to the US when living abroad.

hours to hear from me. I told him yeah, and he said okay. Then I called my friends and let the young lady know that I was 12 hours away.

I settled in and started crying again. I was in a row by myself because the plane wasn't very booked. I was able to stretch out and lay down on the pillow. I had my own extra blanket. All these things were going through my mind. "*What if the plane falls down? What if I will never be able to see my parents again? Why did I do this?*"

There was nothing positive coming into my mind at that time, and then the intercom came on. The stewardess said that in-flight options to use the internet would be activated once we reached a specific altitude. I was excited. I could use my phone or email. It was a beautiful experience. I messaged my mom and dad to let them know that I could talk through the air and that they had cool Wi-Fi during the flight. I was

> **MEDICAL NOTE:**
> Research access to hospitals and healthcare options before planning to move aboard.

able to check in every now and then. We had three meals with real silverware. I got up and walked around to stretch every four hours so that I would not get a blood clot. I watched all types of movies. In between the sections of rows, there was a little service area

MEDICAL NOTE:
When flying over four hours, there is a high risk of blood clots. Compression socks and frequent stretching is recommended.

where you could go and get what you wanted. They had all types of food, snacks like fruit and chocolate delights. They gave you warm towels so you could wash your hands, a toiletry kit that had toothpaste and a toothbrush, socks, and an eye mask. They dimmed the lights. When I woke up to what would have been morning there, they gave me another face-refreshing towel. Being on the plane taught me that there was so much more out there. I was scared, but I had already made the decision and I was going to be okay.

The pilot announced our arrival in Dubai and I began rustling through my papers, trying to remember everything that my employer said. I didn't know anybody, not even this young lady from Facebook, but I had to get processed through immigration. My employer told me I would be met by a greeter. Traditionally in America, when you have a greeter, they find you at baggage claim. In Dubai, the greeter for me was there as soon as I came off the escalator. She was dressed in nice clothing holding up a sign that said, *"Dr. Kentaya Beeler, Welcome."* She said, *"Hello Doctor. I'm so glad to meet you. Welcome to the United Arab Emirates. Everything has been taken care of for you."* There was a baggage hop there and it was almost like they were bowing to me. Everything was "Dr. Kentaya." I couldn't believe it. When the greeter said welcome to me, she also asked if I was traveling alone. I said *"Yes,"* but then I saw the nurse I met while in line boarding in New York. She was from Philadelphia and was moving to Dubai as well. She was nearby, so I said she was with me too and she joined us. They took us through a special line to process our passports so we didn't have to wait. Then they took me through a separate area with all of my luggage. There was someone from the college there to greet me. He introduced himself and said he would be taking care of me. The nurse was with another employer, and so we parted ways.

The gentleman took me to the hotel where I would be staying. He gave me money and meal vouchers and stated that he would come back the next day because they were going to do an orientation for everyone new. When I got to the hotel, I called my parents and friends to let them know I was okay. I told them I was treated like royalty. I knew I wasn't supposed to be excited because I left them all, but if that was how it was going to be, I would never go back. They said okay. I told my parents that I was staying at the Premier Inn Hotel, which was equivalent to a Hilton Garden Inn and Suites. It wasn't upscale, but it was still a decent hotel. That was my whole transition there originally.

The next day, I met about 20 other new hires. I was the only African American female, and I was the only American in the group. Everyone was astonished that I made the journey from America to Dubai. I met people from all over, including Australia, Spain, and the United Kingdom, to name a few. A lot of them had spouses and children with them, and there were a few single people also. They started helping us look for accommodations. I was hired directly by the government of the

United Arab Emirates, and my contract was through them for their actual college, which was equivalent to a community college in the U.S. They spoke to us about our salaries, and mine was equivalent to six figures in the United States. It was tax-free and tax-exempt, and I would be paid monthly. Part of my package included housing, so I received an allotment that was separate from my salary, but I was responsible for finding my own place. The housing money was not immediately made available. Some employers in Dubai have buildings they bring people straight into and give them keys to. My employer was going to give me a check for a year. In Dubai, they pay their rent a year in advance.

Before I arrived, I was told about hotel apartments. It is a hotel with a section of apartments for people who are staying a long time, such as 12-month contractors, while the other side is a regular hotel. The middle had the spa, restaurant, pharmacy, rental cars, tourist excursions, pool, and gym. The rooms came fully furnished and were all-inclusive with internet, water, etc. I went on a tour with everyone to see apartments because the college has relationships with realtors. In the United Arab Emirates, normal apartments have just walls. You have to buy your own appliances including the refrigerator, stove, washer, and dryer. A lot of people have washers, but they do not have dryers. They have old-school clothing lines. Within the first couple of days of looking for places to stay, I recognized a problem. In order for me to get my classes and syllabus together, I didn't have time to look for a place to stay, appliances, or things to furnish it with, such as a bed. That was going to be a challenge for me. In the case of the families that came with spouses who were not working, the spouses could take on that responsibility while we were doing

115

other things. I realized a hotel apartment was better for me. I was about to take a taxi and asked if anybody else wanted to go. One of the couples placed their perceptions of what they thought of African Americans on me. They told me that they understood that I wanted to party, and that's why I preferred to stay in the hotel, but they didn't want that type of lifestyle. I said, *"I want to party? No, I don't want to party. Where did you get that from? I want something that's cost-effective."* They said they knew how we all are. That was my first experience with stereotypes about African Americans from a non-American standpoint. As an African American, it was assumed I was interested in partying, socializing, and not taking life seriously, even though I had a Ph.D.

I took a taxi to a hotel apartment that I had already looked up. I once again experienced the royal treatment. *"Dr. Kentaya, we were waiting for you. This is what's in your budget."* It was equivalent to a one-bedroom, fully furnished condo with all appliances. Inside the hotel corridors were security cameras. The apartment came with a parking space and discounts on the amenities that the hotel offered, and it was move-in ready. All I needed was for my employer to write the check. The problem I faced was transportation. I was told before I came that they had a subway system. Because I had lived in New York, I planned on using the subway, but it only went north and south. The college was more east and west. There was also no train station close to where the college was, so I was going to need a car. If I had moved into the apartments they showed us, those would have been within walking distance. I thought that when I arrived, everything was luxurious until I went outside and it was equivalent to 120 degrees. We were told that we could walk to work from the apartments, but I did not want to walk in that heat. I decided to secure transportation and was told to go back to the airport so I could rent a car as a tourist first because I didn't have an Emirates ID, which is like a government ID for a long-term rental. I could, as an American tourist, use my regular driver's license and rent a car from the airport until my Emirates ID came. There was a teacher special that would allow me to pick up and drop off the car at the airport when I went home for holidays, and that would be a part of the contract, but I couldn't enroll until I had an Emirates ID. I did go back and get a car as a tourist.

I soon learned that an Emirates ID was critical to conducting business in Dubai. It was needed when moving into an apartment to establish utilities, cable, and water, which they call DEWA. All new hires were told the hotel was paid for 14 days, but we were not able to turn on utilities or anything else until we had our Emirates ID. It was needed to move into an apartment. The great thing was that I didn't need that ID to move into the hotel apartment, so it was indeed a better fit for me. As the details of getting settled emerged, there was a big uproar. That was my first experience realizing everything in writing is not always clear in Dubai. They never explained that the hotel would be for 14 days and that it's possible you would need to cover another week to 10 days on your own until you could move out into an apartment.

I was frustrated. What was I supposed to do? I had no money before graduation. I spent a lot of money to relocate and didn't have extra money to pay for a hotel. I went to HR and told them I couldn't afford another week. I wanted to move into a hotel apartment and it was available, but they had not yet written the check to cover the stay because they only issued checks once a month. I didn't realize that HR didn't allow loud talking, arguments, or disagreements. I was being American. I told them it was ridiculous. Why would we have to pay? Everybody was looking at me with an *"Are you stupid?"* expression. I couldn't be there, raising my voice.

There was a local Emirati woman working for my employer, who said, *"Let me help you. Just calm down. I have family in the U.S., and I understand your point of view, but you can't state your level of disagreement at that volume, and you have to reword it."* She said that she would help me out because I wasn't going to get assistance acting like that. I said that she was absolutely right. She told me that the college knew this in advance, but they didn't tell me. What I needed to say was that I needed help. She told me to say, *"I need help with my hotel stay because I can't afford to pay for my living until the check is provided."* She told me if I said I needed help, it would come across differently. I told her, *"Are you kidding me?* From that day to this day, she has been a friend almost like a sister. She made sure the room was paid for every day. She said that is what I had to do, and she could only do it for me, even though that may have seemed wrong. Every day I had to go there and remind her to call the hotel to extend the hotel stay for about five days. Then they wrote the check, and I went to live in the hotel apartment.

I enjoyed my accommodations, and they were paid for a year in advance. That was my first time not looking to pay bills at a certain time because they were already covered. I was being exposed to something new. My salary was divided by

12 and directly deposited into my account at the beginning of the month. Someone cleaned my room twice a week. When I wanted room service or anything else, it was always a pleasure. It was very different from America. Staff were always so pleased to serve. I've never experienced that in America. They were so happy that I came to their country to work, and they respected my educational accomplishments as well as how I treated them. What I learned was that most people were from other countries and were sacrificing as well to provide a better life for their families, so we were all even in that regard. However, I discovered because I was American, I was making much more than many of my colleagues. This was because in Dubai, you are paid based on your passport and the standard cost of living in your home country. The reality is, I didn't get any job offers after I received my Ph.D. in America. I was sacrificing because I wanted something new.

THE LESSON

The highlight of my offer and relocation to the United Arab Emirates was learning, unlearning, and relearning. I learned that there was a life more beautiful than I knew outside the United States. I had to learn some new cultural norms, like not raising my voice when I needed help but asking that nicely for assistance instead. I also learned how to dress like them. I learned that people have a different and stereotypical opinion of African Americans, and I didn't like what I discovered.

The most important lesson I believe you should get from this is that you need to learn to know when to leave your comfort zone and be comfortable doing it. Trust me, it's not going to be easy leaving your already established life, your home, and your loved ones. It might even be more difficult if you have a spouse and kids. I believe that the decision to leave was a bit easier for me because I was single. If I'd had a family, I'm not sure I would have accepted the offer at all. There will come a moment in your life when you will be required to leave your comfort zone for something better. The zone can become so comfortable that you stop moving forward and just remain in one position. At that point, leaving your comfort zone may be what you need.

I know we always talk about being selfless and all, but there will come a time when you will need to be selfish. You will need to think about yourself and what makes you happy. You can talk to people and get advice from them, but at the end of the day, the decision-making lies with you. You can't make a decision based on how other people will feel, but on how you will feel. I love my mom so much but at that point, I just couldn't stay back because she was concerned about my past health battles and sad about me leaving. I had to take the offer for myself and not anyone else. Eventually, she came around, and guess what? She even came to visit me in Dubai! Everyone was happy.

66 WHEN THE TIME COMES FOR ME TO MAKE A TOUGH DECISION, I WILL DO WHAT'S BEST FOR ME. I WILL ALWAYS BE A CHAMPION OF MYSELF. 99

HAVE A SEAT AT THE TABLE 9

GONE BUT NOT FORGOTTEN

THE STORY

"My dad loved fishing and I knew that he was with the Master of the Sea!" ~ Dr. Kentaya Beeler

DURING MY SUMMER BREAK IN 2017, I TRAVELED BACK home. My dad had prostate cancer around 2009, and he said the tumor was removed when they took out his prostate. My dad revealed that the cancer had come back. He was getting treatment, but in the summer of 2017, it had progressed into bone cancer. The prostate cancer came back looking for the prostate and because it was not there, the cancer spread to the tailbone and then his back. My dad built golf courses and had endured back surgery and shoulder surgery. He thought the pain that he was feeling in his back was from the past surgery. I went to some appointments with my dad, and unbeknownst to me, he had decided not to continue to get the radiation injections in his back. He said the injection site hurt worse than the pain he was feeling from the cancer. I also came to know that he was not getting his **PSA levels**

MEDICAL NOTE:
The PSA test is a blood test used primarily to screen for prostate cancer. The test measures the amount of prostate-specific antigen (PSA) in your blood.

tested annually. The pain was starting to spread through his body because the cancer was in his bones. I talked to him about whether I should stay in America, and he said no because he was married, had support, and they would keep me in the loop. He had one more pain management appointment before I was to return to Dubai and he asked me to attend because he said the pain was beginning to get unbearable all over his body.

When we got there, a young West African doctor was assigned to oversee his pain management. My dad had to do blood and urine tests in the laboratory, which was located in the office. When the doctor wanted to tell us about the test results, he said, *"Well Ms. Beeler, can you come inside?"* and my dad said, *"No, her name is Dr. Beeler."* The doctor said, *"Okay, so Dr. Beeler, you are familiar with your dad's condition."* I said no that I had a Ph.D. and not an M.D. I told him that I knew that my dad had bone cancer and he was having pain and they were saying that was from him no longer receiving radiation shots. The doctor explained that when you stop taking the radiation injection, over time the cancer will be more painful than the radiation injection. Also, my dad's increased pain was because the cancer had spread. The doctor turned to my father and said, *"But do you want me to tell your daughter what your results are right now in your urine and your blood?"* My dad told him to go ahead. *"I'm transparent with my daughter, and I tell her everything."* He told me, *"Dr. Beeler, your dad came in here dirty."* I said, *"What's dirty?"* He said, *"Your dad has cocaine in his system."*

I was like, *"Huh?"* My dad said, *"Well, you tell her why I got cocaine in my system."* The doctor said, *"Well, I don't know. You tell her."* My dad told me, *"Baby, I have cocaine in my system because it numbs the pain, and people need to know that before cocaine was illegal, it was used as a pain medicine. I'm tired of going back and forth with these doctors about pain medicine. I'm allergic to certain pain medicines and you and I have to suffer, baby girl, because of our allergies. They don't look at my allergies in advance, and they give me stuff like oxycontin. I break out in rashes and things like that, so I had no choice but to go to the street because I'm tired of being in pain."* I was dumbfounded and asked, *"Doc, is this true?"* The doctor said, *"That's true. Cocaine used to be used for pain, but we know what cocaine does to other parts of the body. Right now, his heart rate is so high that his heart could explode. So, the cocaine is going to numb the pain, but I'm more scared that he is going to die from a heart attack because he already has high blood pressure and then he is using the cocaine for pain management."* He said that he could give my dad pain medicine that was within his allergy restrictions. Then he said, *"I'm going to tell you and your daughter that there is nothing I will ever be able to prescribe that will equate to what cocaine does, and that is the harsh reality. The other part of it is today, I can't do anything for you. I can't give you any medicine knowing that you currently have cocaine in your system. You will have to go off of cocaine for a complete seven days with no trace of it in your system before I would, for malpractice risk, give you any pain medicine."*

My dad looked at me and wanted to know what I wanted him to do. He said, *"At this point, I'm dying. There's nothing they can do for me, so what do you want me to do?"* I said, *"What?"* He asked what I wanted him to do. Did I want him to stop the cocaine and just go through the pain for seven days and take the prescribed pain medicine, or did I want him to continue the cocaine? He said he would die either from bone cancer or a heart attack, but he was leaving it to me. I had never in my life been faced with a decision like that. I said, *"I don't know how to do that."* My dad said, *"Well, you're going to make the decision."* Then he got up and walked out. Left in the room were me, the doctor, and my uncle, who went after my dad to talk to him.

The doctor said that he couldn't do anything without my dad there and asked if he could just come back. When he returned, my dad said, *"Kentaya, what do you want because you are sitting there with tears in your eyes. What do you want me to do?"* I told him that I wanted him to get off the cocaine and try the pain medicine. He said, *"Okay, I'll do it."* The doctor said, *"Mr. Beeler, that's going cold turkey."* My dad said, *"I'll go cold turkey. I'll do anything for my baby. If she wants me to go cold turkey, I'll go cold turkey."* As we went out that day, the doctor said to me, *"You seem like a very smart girl, and I don't want you to be disappointed. It's highly unlikely that he'll be able to go cold turkey. When they come off of cocaine, the impact of the pain is so massive that they're going to go into withdrawals. They are going to go back to that.*"

Fast forward, we went back in seven days and completed the same process. My dad got his blood drawn and his urinalysis done. We went in to see the doctor, and I saw this big smile on his face. He looked at me and said that my dad had proven him wrong. He said, *"I'm going to tell you, for real, straight up, Mr. Beeler. I told Dr. Beeler that you were not going to be able to do it. It is very rare that we see this. Your dad is clean! He has no drugs in his system. I'm ready, sir. I have your prescription, but I do want to have this conversation with you. This is not going to stop you from having pain, this is just going to diminish the impact of pain."* He asked if I knew my dad was terminal. *"We can prolong his life by reducing the spread of bone cancer, but bone cancer is one of the most painful terminal illnesses at this time. He can live for years with bone cancer, but the pain is insurmountable. We can still put him on radiation injections, but it has spread a lot."*

When we left there, I was really impacted by the word "terminal." My dad said, *"I told you I'm dying."* I told him, *"Daddy, but you say we all die every day."* He said, *"Yeah, but there ain't nothing they can do for me."* I told him that he could get back on the radiation. He said he wasn't going to be doing that. *"It hurts, so if I'm just going to be in pain, let me just be in pain. Don't just keep me here and keep spreading it out."* I said, *"Do you want me to stay?"* He said, *"No, because it could be years."* There was something in me that knew it wasn't going to be years, but I didn't know how long. That was in August of 2017.

I decided to book one of his favorite activities, which was a half-day fishing charter trip along with a hotel stay on St. Pete beach for me and him. It was a magical weekend. He was so excited when I told him we had a daughter-dad date. We caught about 20 fish. Some we threw back into the sea because of their size, and the others we kept to take home. That weekend we walked the beach, laughed a lot, and debated about what was on the news. It felt like old times when I was a child and it was me and him in the garage listening to his eight-tracks. He would pull out our headphones so we could nod our heads together. That's where I learned from an early age that his favorite song was from Marvin Gaye, *Got to give it up*. He loved Curtis Mayfield too. That weekend felt good.

When I went back to Dubai, I would call him and he wouldn't answer much. I would call his wife, and she would say he was tired. We were skyping, and then we weren't anymore. In October 2017, I wanted to Skype for my birthday but he wouldn't. That was strange, and by the end of October, I got frustrated. I told him that he was going to Skype with me. I didn't understand why he wasn't answering my phone calls. He would call when I was working and just leave voicemails. I didn't understand why he was calling just to leave a message. Finally, his wife said, *"Kentaya, your daddy told me not to tell you, but your daddy can't even walk anymore. He is in a hospital bed, and he doesn't want you to see him like that."* I didn't understand what she was talking about. We had just gone to the doctor and on a fishing trip. She told me, *"I'm just going to leave that to him because you know how he is or whatever because it is you. Let him explain to you."*

I said, *"Okay."* I said to him, *"Hey daddy, do you have something you've got to tell me?"* He said, *"Yeah, you know one day I fell? I haven't been able to get up since. They said they can't do nothing else for me."* I said, *"What do you mean you fell and you can't get up?"* Then he said, *"Kentaya, I don't want to talk about it. I don't want to Skype."* I said, *"Okay."* Two days later, he texted me and told me that he was in the hospital. He was ranting and raving. I had voicemails from him that said to call the police and the sheriff's department because they tried taking advantage of him and he couldn't call for himself. I called back the number, and then a nurse said, *"Miss, your daddy threw piss at me. He's throwing objects in the room."* I asked why he was in the hospital, and she told me that he had a bed sore and pneumonia. I was confused. *"My daddy?"* She told me *"Yes."* I wanted to know why no one called me. I told her that he was telling me to call the police. She said that they told him that they were going to strap him down if he didn't stop. I wanted to talk to him, but he told me not to talk to him and to talk to the doctors.

I spoke to the doctors and recorded the conversation. They told me they were giving my dad six months to live because his condition was deteriorating. There was nothing else that they could do for him, and he didn't like anything they tried. The moisture on his back caused the infection, which caused the fever and cold, which caused him to get pneumonia, and that was why he was hospitalized. They were going to set him up for hospice care. I then made the decision that I was going home. I asked if I had enough time until December, and they told me that I did.

I went back to my employer and asked for a leave of absence because I signed a three-year contract but had only worked 18 months. They told me no because I had signed a contract. I would have to pay back the money I had received. I told them that my dad was sick. They asked, *"What kind of sick?"* I told them that he had cancer. They told me they would have to see if I could get a leave, and they asked if I had read my contract. I had read it. I was so upset. I knew I didn't have enough to pay them back the real money I was making at this job in Dubai. I read the contract again and it said that for terminal illnesses, if you are the direct caregiver, you may be given an exception. I told them that I was his only child who lived in Florida. I was considered an only child even though he had other children, but I had never met them. They took my passport to make sure I didn't flee and so they could do an investigation. They would let me know if I would be eligible for an exception. They told me, *"Understand we spent a lot of money on recruiting you over here, and we don't have anybody else with a Ph.D. in accounting on our staff. In our custom, we bury within 24 hours. In the policy, we will allow you four days."* Four days! It would take me a day to get to the U.S. and a day to come back. What's four days? I wanted to be there because they gave my dad six months. I wanted to take leave and come back later.

They told me, *"No, we don't do it like that because death is a part of life."* I told them that as Americans, traditionally we don't have services for two weeks. They said that two weeks was not respectful in Muslim culture. They cannot hold a body out for more than 24 hours, and it can't surpass noon the next day. Now this was the cultural difference coming into play through my contract. I told the HR representative handling my case what was happening in my department, and she said that she would give me my passport back if I had an emergency. In order to cover herself, she would keep it there. She gave me her mobile number. Around seven days later, they came back and said that they would let me out of the contract. I received so much retaliation at work for it. People hated me. Some of the other coworkers and professors were saying that they would have to pick up my slack because I was leaving and I had been writing the curriculum. They said I was brought there to write tax curriculum and I was leaving them. All the while I kept saying, *"My dad is dying, and I told you I would be back. I can't focus because of what's going on with my dad. The time difference and not being able to answer the phone in the classroom was an issue. My daddy needed me, and he was calling me to talk about calling the police."* My supervisor, who had traditionally been good to me, said, *"I'm disappointed in you. You know that we all sacrificed to be here in this country, and a lot of us have missed our parents' funerals. We missed important birthdays, anniversaries, and kids' graduations back in our home countries. This is very selfish of you."* Everything became very toxic and horrible. I finally made arrangements to leave. In my mind, I knew I was going to come back to Dubai because I liked the lifestyle. I just didn't know when. The people who understood me were those with whom I had made friends with. I left a lot of my things at their houses in Dubai just so I could have the basic two suitcases to take home.

The plane couldn't fly fast enough and the car ride from Orlando seemed slow, but I finally arrived at my dad's house. I went inside his home, and I found my dad in the bed dirty. His shirt was soiled with spaghetti from a dish that was half flipped over. He was in a sedated state, trying to feed himself. He was in an adult diaper, and he barely recognized me. I was heartbroken by his condition. The room had diapers and sterile wipes stacked to the ceiling. It looked like a medical room in the house, and he was in a hospital bed. Dirt had accumulated on his forehead, so it looked like he had a burn mark. My aunt, my mom, and I were there. His wife wasn't there but her daughter was. She was supposed to be watching him, but she was outside. Then she came inside and said that he was eating, and she didn't know how he had gotten like that. I looked at her, and I just looked at my dad, and I didn't say anything. I saw a pink basin bowl, and I went to get some water and realized there was no hot water. I tried the kitchen sink, and the water was still cold. My aunt and I just changed his shirt and I saw his eyes looking at me. He was trying to focus, then he said, *"Hey baby."* I said *"Hey"* back and then he semi dozed off. My aunt started to sing and he started to clap. We began singing gospel music because my dad loved to sing. It was at that moment it hit me. This was real. I was not prepared to see him that way.

I lived an hour-and-a-half away from my dad at my mom's house. I hadn't driven my car in two years, but I could drive to see my dad. I soon realized that my dad was going through elder abuse, and his wife was the abuser. She was his fifth wife, but also his third. He had left her for another lady before, and she took him back, but then he got sick. She was angry at me for coming because I was holding her accountable. The first thing I asked of her was to stop over sedating him. That was the way that they were handling him so that during the day when she was at work, he would be in a sedated state. I offered to help pay for a home healthcare aid to come and care for my father while his wife was at work, but she told me no. She had it covered, and didn't want anyone in her house. I ordered an internal independent review from my dad's medical doctor to come out and see him. We had a family meeting. My dad had a level-four ulcer on his back, so the pain he was feeling wasn't from bone cancer alone. It was because he was being neglected and mistreated by his wife and her daughters. I expressed my concern in front of the doctor. He said that the ulcer came from not turning him. While he spoke, his wife just sat there. I was never given the opportunity to spend the night at their home, nor would I want to, so I just drove home. I got there, and his wife's daughter wrote me this long letter on Facebook about how my dad mistreated her mama. She said that I didn't see what her mama went through, that I was "Johnny come lately" and wanted to be "Captain Save A Hoe." She said that my dad was exchanging his oxycontin for cocaine on the street and that I didn't have the right to question the treatment of my father at that moment.

> **WEDGE-BEDSORE RESCUE** is a turning wedge that takes the pressure off of the spine

I left a toxic environment at work to come to a toxic environment with my dad. I had to walk on eggshells just to spend time with him. Then, as he started to wean off the medicine, he had honest conversations with me about his mistreatment in the house and what was going on.

It came to a boiling point, and my dad said, *"My daughter can come here, f*** y'all. You're not going to make her feel unwelcome because y'all have been treating me like s*** and now somebody's come here to reveal what I haven't been able to reveal. If y'all got a problem with that, then take it out on me like you've been. If she wants to come here, she can come here. If she wants me to have Egyptian silk sheets on my bed, she can. If she wants me to go exercising, that's what I am going to do."* I ordered him a **hoyer lift** and set up time so we could video chat. I got him a nutribullet so he could make a shake out of Ensure. They had been giving him Wendy's frosties even though he was borderline diabetic and sugar makes cancer cells spread. During our visits, we had pizza parties and played games. We did puzzles together like we did when I was a child, which made his wife and her daughters angry.

HOYER LIFT–A Hoyer lift is a patient lift used by caregivers to safely transfer patients. It can be used for lifting patients from the floor or onto a healthcare bed. The lift also can assist in other surface-to-surface patient transfers, such as moving from a bed to a bath or chair.

Dr. Beeler & Dad

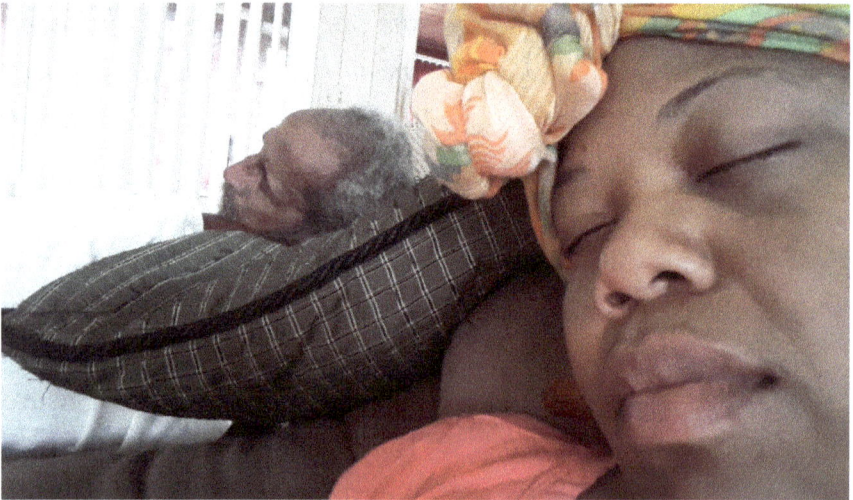

One particular day, he was resting and I was at his bedside watching TV. I heard him clear his throat and he turned his head toward me, *"Kentaya, promise me one thing."* I said, *"What's that?"* He said, *"Be who you are."* I said, *"Huh? What do you mean by that?"* He said, *"Never change who you are for*

nobody. You are an amazing person, let alone a woman, and people don't like that. But no matter what, if there is anything that you can do for me, be who you are. And as I always say, if anybody don't like you, f*** him! Be who you are, baby." I said in a childlike tone, *"Okay daddy."* He opened his eyes and said, *"I'm serious, baby girl."* We both laughed and I said, *"I know you are."* He went on to say, *"Kentaya, I'm about to leave you, and I can no longer protect you like I have always done. I am going home with my God very soon, but I know that you are strong enough to handle the battles. I've protected you from a lot of things and people and you will soon see that everyone around you is not for you. So just be who you are and know that your daddy loves you."* In return, I tried to convince him to put down his wishes for death in writing like his DNR and living will, but he refused. He said, *"I ain't going to be here, so put my ass in the corner. I want you and my wife to work that out."* Was he delirious? They were not working with me then. He told me that he didn't want me to be doing all that crying either at his services. I wanted him to understand that if he did not put it in writing, I had no rights. He insisted that he wanted me and his wife to work together. On February 14, Valentine's Day, we had a good time on video chat and he looked good. On February 15, I got a call that they took him to the hospice center because he was sick, throwing up, and barely responsive. I told them that I would be right there, so I jumped in the car with my mom and I went there.

As I rushed through the halls, I passed all these rooms with people with their mouths open. They looked stuck, but like they couldn't close them. Their arms were stretched out. It

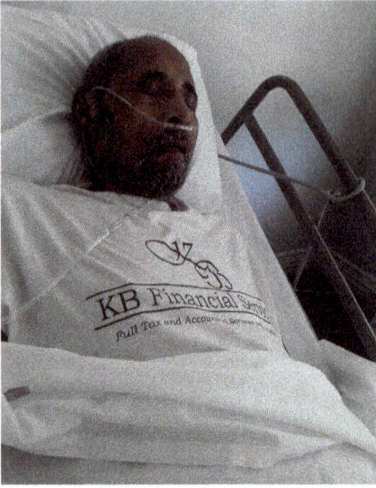

was very dark, and people were crying, but the hospice center location had beautiful grounds. They told me that they sent people there for end of life 24-hour medical care until they passed. I went into the room, and he was just lying there. His wife was commenting to me that he was half conscious, but he told her to put on him this shirt. It was for me. I looked down, and it was my very first accounting firm shirt, KB Financial Services. He was adamant about wearing that shirt. He was just lying there, so I said, *"Can you hear me? If you can hear me, move your hand."* He didn't move his hand at all. I held his hand, and it was really soft but not cold. I knew he was still there and that he was in a subconscious state.

I stayed a couple of hours. My mom remained in the car and when I went back, I just broke down. I couldn't believe it. Two months! It had only been two months. I had just returned home in December. We were doing so well with all the exercise. How did all of this happen? I went back home, and then his wife called and said that somebody wanted to talk to me. This was on February 16. I heard him say, *"Hey baby."* I said, *"Hey!"* He asked, *"What are you doing?"* I asked him, *"What are you doing?"* He said he was drinking apple juice. The day before, I questioned if they were going to feed him because he didn't look like he had been eating. They told me they don't force anyone to eat or drink in hospice. Patients have to do it on their own. I said, *"He could starve to death."* The lady said, *"Yeah. We are not going to force him to eat."* I was so upset. Imagine, to my surprise, the next day when he was sitting up drinking apple juice. I said, *"Oh my God."* I told him I would be there, and it took me 45 minutes. He was laying in the bed, but they had him propped up. There was a whole lot of family there, including my dad's sisters and brothers and his wife. Then she said for everyone to clear the room because I was there. My dad said, *"That's right."* We talked, and he drank. I asked if he remembered hearing me from the day before, and he told me no. He didn't remember hearing anybody, and I said, *"Oh."* He said, *"Yeah. they say I'm supposed to go home tomorrow."* I said, *"Go home tomorrow?"* He said, *"Yeah."* The nurse came and I repeated, *"He's supposed to go home tomorrow?"* She also said, *"Yeah. Hospice is for the end of life but he's bounced back and he's doing a phenomenal job."* In my heart, I didn't want him to go back to that house, but I didn't say anything. We sat there and we talked. He didn't eat anything, but he was drinking. He said he wasn't hungry. Then I remembered that I had a knee appointment that day. I told my daddy that I needed to go back to Tampa before they closed, but that he had a lot of company. He said *"Yeah"* and that they were going to have a good old time. There was a patio and everybody was out there watching TV. I walked out of the room and I said, *"I love you."* He said, *"I love you more."* I said, *"No, I love you more."* He said, *"Naw girl, I love you more"* and he blew a kiss. I got to the door and it was an awkward feeling. I just looked back at him and he went back to sleep. His wife was calling his name, "Harry, Harry." She said he wasn't going to do anymore talking that day because he had talked to who HE wanted to!

When I was walking out, I went back and asked if there was any way that he could be transported somewhere else tomorrow. I didn't want him to go back to that house. I asked the nurse if she saw the level-four ulcer on his back. She said yeah but explained that the spouse has the ultimate rights to make decisions. *"If you, as his daughter, don't have power of attorney, he will have to go back to his home,"* she said. *"I'm sorry, dear."* This sounded familiar from my brain surgery preparation and was the primary reason why I expedited my divorce. Now here I was dealing with this same issue with my father. I walked out the door, and I called back that night. His wife said that he had been sleeping since I left and that he was doing pretty well. She told me that they were supposed to get ready to send him home the next day and that she wasn't spending the night because she stayed the night before. On February 17, 2018, I woke up in the morning and called his wife. He was still sleeping, so they would play it by ear. They didn't know if he was going to go home. She said he was nothing like yesterday. I told her that I would be up there later but was going to see *Black Panther* with friends and family. While in the movie, my phone started blowing up. I ignored it, then it started blowing up again. I went outside, and it was my dad's wife's sister on the phone to let me know that my dad had passed away. He never woke up and passed in his sleep. She asked me if I wanted them to hold the body for me to come see him. I wasn't sure at that moment. I went somewhere outside of my body. Then she said they were going to call the science place, and they would pick him up from hospice. I said, *"What science place? What people?"* She told me to talk to his wife. She said she thought she told me that my dad donated his body to science. I said, *"What? Donated his body to science?"* She said, *"Yeah, hospice will do a free cremation if you donate your body to science, so your dad and I agreed on it."* I said, *"When? What about a funeral?"* She said, *"No we won't be having no body at no funeral. That's neither here nor there. Do you want to come see him, or can I just have them come pick him up?"* I was in St. Pete and it was going to take me about an hour from where I was. I said, *"No, I don't want to see him after rigor mortis has set in. No, it's okay. I choose to still see him from yesterday, when we were talking."* She said, *"Okay, that's fine."* That was the last time I saw my dad. On February 24, 2018, I decided to have a seaside memorial at St. Pete beach, the same place that we took our last fishing trip, and called it "Harry's gone fishing." My dad loved fishing, and I knew that he was with the Master of the Sea!

THE LESSON

My family members have had their fair share of illnesses, and it hurt to watch my dad go through so much pain from cancer and abuse from his wife. I wish I had more power to do something, but I had no authority to take action. I could only help and love him from a distance. This again boils down to the fact that you should carefully choose who you decide to do life with. You have to trust that the person you're giving the power to will come through for you when the time comes. My dad wasn't perfect, but I believe that he deserved more than what he got when he was dying.

I'm not sure my dad transitioned the way he preferred, but he did live an exciting life. We can all learn to create our own excitement. Relocate if you have to, challenge yourself, try out a new career, travel the world if you have the means, and be happy because when you are transitioning, it is those memories that you have to hold on to. To top all of these, I'm happy that my dad and I had a great relationship before he died. There are no regrets beside the fact that I wish we had published our cooking book that we talked about since he was a wonderful cook, and that he would have documented his end-of-life desires in writing. I will cherish all of our memories and wonderful moments with him before he went to eternal sleep.

"Make sure you prepare to transition the way you desire. Everyone deserves a celebration of life!"

CONCLUSION

KEEP YOU FIRST

"You must be a champion of yourself at every table that you sit at in life. Keep you first." ~ Dr. Kentaya Beeler

AFTER MY FATHER FELL ILL, MY CHOICE TO LEAVE DUBAI was not one I had to think twice about. The stakes were high, as the company I worked for at the time held firmly that if I made the decision to leave, I would no longer be a part of their organization. Had this decision not been a matter of life and death, it is possible that I would have considered the prospect of returning to Dubai. My career was taking off and for the first time in a long time, I was back on my feet. In retrospect, the gift is in knowing today that I was by my father's side for the last two months of his life. My satisfaction is in knowing that I did what needed to be done in the best interest of my family.

Today, I work full-time online for a university in the United States. I still run my accounting firm and I have since launched a non-profit organization with an emphasis on education. We have active programming in Africa as well as the United States. Over the last several years, our advocacy has evolved to ensure the support of families and planning for the series of events that take place during life and death. I founded CHAMOMÈ,

LLC, a company that specializes in educating families on essential areas of life planning to foster effective decision-making skills, resulting in an enhanced quality of life. I also run a travel agency purposed to expose individuals to new outlooks on life and destinations traveled. After venturing to Dubai, Sri Lanka, and Africa, I knew without question I wanted to establish avenues for others to see the world.

My continued message to the world is that life planning is essential and to remind everyone that life will have curve balls. The goal is to be as prepared as possible when they are thrown. I'm not as naive today as I was when I was younger because of life's circumstances. There was a time when I felt like I could control a great part of my life. Although we have the power to make critical decisions about our lives, there will never be a time when we have total control. Acknowledging this fact allowed me to learn three of the greatest lessons of my lifetime:

1. **Trust God. It is in Him and only Him that we access total control.**
2. **You can never control anyone else's response to who you are, but be you each and every day.**
3. **Our parents were given the assignment to birth us, but we have no right to judge how they carried out their assignment.**

If you remember nothing else that I have written about, never forget what championing and advocating for yourself looks like. It's not necessarily pretty, but necessary. I want families to communicate more about their finances and expectations of each other when it comes to health and caregivers. Who is expected to carry out the wishes of another? The dash between birth and death is uncertain. Therefore, we must take the time to make the best of life. The mark you leave on Earth is left to you to work on daily.

I KEEP IT ALL TOGETHER

I Keep It All
Together Project

THE "I KEEP IT ALL TOGETHER" PROJECT IS AN INITIATIVE born out of the lived experiences of Dr. Kentaya Beeler, the founder of CHAMOMÉ, LLC who is a brain tumor survivor and who has been a caregiver for her mother during a season of acute illness and her late father.

The "I Keep It All Together" Project is comprised of a portal that will assist families in life planning. The portal is an online communication platform for subscribers to maintain their medical records, organize their end-of-life preparations, and maintain their financial affairs. Equipped with a secure username and password, subscribers gain anytime access to their records from the comfort of their home or the mobile app. This accessibility provides comfort for families, caregivers, and single individuals seeking to achieve organization of their life in one location.

The CHAMOMÉ, LLC Portal is powered by Harris Health, an electronic medical record system that is licensed and HIPAA-compliant to ensure data security.

WWW.CHAMOME.COM
WWW.IKEEPITALLTOGETHER.COM

ABOUT THE AUTHOR

"Public service must be more than doing a job efficiently and honestly. It must be a complete dedication to the people and to the nation." ~ Margaret Chase Smith

Dr. Kentaya Beeler knows and lives a life of purpose and public service. It's a life that she grew to know all too well as a young adult dealing with severe health challenges; both personally and with her parents. A native of St. Petersburg, Florida, Dr. Beeler holds a B.S. in Accounting from Florida A&M University, Masters in Taxation from Nova Southeastern University, and a Ph.D. in Business with a specialization in Accounting from Capella University. Her dissertation, aptly entitled, "Families' Decisions to Purchase Long-Term Care Insurance and Relevant Tax Deductions," was based on her personal experiences dealing with the healthcare system.

Dr. Beeler's extensive and diverse work experience began in New York City, where she worked as an external auditor of financial institutions for a subsidiary of the State of New

York Department of Treasury. A relocation back to her home state in 2004 led her to accept a position as an internal auditor for a publicly traded construction company in Orlando and two years later, she transitioned into the public accounting industry as a Tax Accountant.

Reflecting on her experiences in undergraduate and graduate school and eager to expand her horizons, Dr. Beeler took her talents to the higher education field and became an Accounting Professor, which she still does to this day. After obtaining her Doctorate in 2016, she was recruited by the government of Dubai, UAE where she developed business course curriculum. This new program covered tax accounting in efforts to prepare for the implementation of the VAT tax in the first GCC country and to prepare Arabic students to work in the future economy of Dubai. She also developed a program with the Ford Motor Company of the Middle East that fostered a pipeline for private industry jobs for Emirati female students seeking business degrees.

Dr. Beeler is also an entrepreneur and an advocate for financial awareness and self-sustainability. The financial expertise she gained through her personal and professional career brought birth to CHAMOMÈ, LLC and the "I Keep It All Together" project. "I Keep It All Together" is an initiative born out of Beeler's lived experiences as a Brain Tumor survivor and a caregiver for her mother during a season of acute illness and her late father who passed from Bone Cancer.

Before creating CHAMOMÈ, LLC., she has owned and operated Tables of Purpose, a non-profit; Traquilpathways Travel and The Balanced Accounting Group. An active member of her community, she has hosted and presented at several conferences on a myriad of topics, but specifically on accounting, budgeting and personal success through money management. Among the many awards that Dr. Beeler has received over her career, receiving the "Women that Win, Financial & Community in Leadership" award in 2017 sticks out the most. "To be recognized for providing my community with the tools that they need to live a fiscally successful life is more than I could ever bargain for," Dr. Beeler said. "We all deserve to live happy and whole lives and all people need is the access to those tools to do it."

Dr. Kentaya Beeler currently resides in Florida. In her free time, she travels, reads novels and fashion magazines and enjoys time with close friends.

NOTES